CUSCO

AND THE SACRED VALLEY

OF THE INCAS

TANKAR EIRL

CUSCO - PERU

Cusco y el Valle Sagrado de los Incas
Cusco and the Sacred Valley of the Incas

Fernando E. Elorrieta Salazar.
Edgar Elorrieta Salazar.

© Fernando E. Elorrieta Salazar.
Edgar Elorrieta Salazar.

Primera edición 2005
Segunda edición, 12ª. reimpresión

Año 2016.   3,000 Ejemplares

Translations: Beverly Nelson Elder

Illustrations: Alfonso Anticona L.
Carlos Olazábal Rodriguez
Martín Manrrique Villalobos
José Luis Morales Sierra

Photographs: Fernando E. Elorrieta Salazar.
Edgar Elorrieta Salazar.
Servicio Aerofotográfico Nacional
Instituto Geográfico Militar de Bolivia

Hecho el Depósito Legal en la Biblioteca Nacional del Perú N° 2016-08145

© TANKAR E.I.R.L.
Alameda Norte s/n Calca, Cusco.
Telf.: 0051-984-685268

Email: fernandoelorrieta@hotmail.com
edgarelorrieta@hotmail.com

www.cuscomachupicchuonbooks.com

Pre-Prensa e Impresión: Ausonia S.A.
Jr. Francisco Lazo 1700 – Lima

ISBN: 978-603-45091-1-5

INDEX

THE GEOGRAPHY

The Andes is the largest of all the mountain ranges in the world. Anchored at Cape Horn in Tierra del Fuego in the southernmost part of Chile and Argentina, it follows the west coast of South America, creating a dense mountainous barrier of high peaks and volcanos along its 7,500 kilometers before finally becoming lost in the sea of the Antilles and the plains of Venezuela.

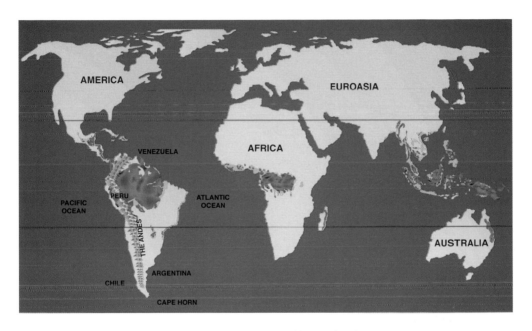

The Andes mountains, Peru, skirting
the Earth's tropical forests.

Peru is located where this colossal mountain chain enters the tropics, but it is still in an area where glaciers contribute to the climate: with cold, which dissipates as the altitude diminishes, and with water, which fertilizes the high, steep slopes and provides, as in few places on the planet, a wide variety of climates and ecosystems. These, scattered like islands in a kind of vast and descending archipelago, lead down one flank of the Andes into the delicate and humid tropical Amazon forest, while descending down the other flank these varied micro-climates are finally buried among the arid valleys of the coastal deserts.

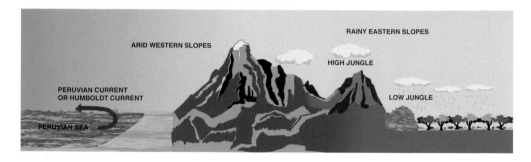

This high, tangled mountain barrier stops the dense clouds that rise from the Amazon and keeps them from refreshing the hot sands of the extremely dry deserts along the Pacific coast. These desert areas are even drier because of the cold, rich oceab water of the Humboldt current, which lowers the temperature and makes rain less likely. However, this cold current occasionally gives way to the hot current of El Niño, causing the climate in the Andes to change. Heavy rainfall in the north then results in overflowing rivers and flooding, while the southern part of the country languishes in a prolonged drought. It is estimated that this regular event happens every three or four years, while every eight to fifteen years it occurs with devastating intensity. Thus the geography of the Andes and the variety of climates to be found here fostered the appearance of an astonishing natural diversity[1] in one of the most demanding terrains on the Planet.[2]

To an altitude of 600 masl. (meters above sea level) the climate is tropical, corn and cotton[3] are the principal crops. On the slopes of the eastern jungles, the fauna is represented by innumerable forest animals, among them the American alligator, the jaguar and the boa.

---

(1) There are 1,710 species of birds that have been identified, 460 mammals, 330 amphibians, more than 17,000 species of plants and so many insects that all are not yet counted. The Office of Evaluation of Natural Resources in Peru (ONERN) identified 81 of natural life and 17 of a transitional nature.

(2) At the moment in Peru only 3.81% of its territory is apt for cultivation. ONERN, Classification of the lands of Peru, 1982 (Annex II:I)

(3) The cotton varieties *Gossypium hirsutum* (Mexico) and *G. Barbadense peruvianum* are indigenous to the Americas. The existence of acclimatized cultivars of cotton at 2,850 masl. in the Sacred Valley of the Incas was recorded in 1552. Rev. del Archivo Histórico del Cusco, no. 13: 39

A Jaguar forms the handle of a Inca ceremonial vessel*; this painting was found at the edge of the jungle, to the east of Cusco (Lares).

Coca.
Erythroxylum coca.

The coca plant grows vigorously to an altitude of 1,800 masl. A shrub that grows up to three meters tall, it produces small red fruits and a foliage of oval leaves with smooth borders which, once dried, are chewed to momentarily alleviate the sensation of fatigue and hunger. The leaves contain carotene, riboflavin, thiamin, iron, and calcium, while among its alkaloids, besides cocaine, it has "ecgonine, an active component of atropine, an element that helps digestion and the assimilation of carbohydrates, which are, as is well known, the mainstay of the diet of Andean peoples."[4] It is also known that chewing the leaves or drinking an infusion of coca "tea" alleviates the effects of altitude sickness (*soroche*), helping to relax the airways to the lungs and restore tone to the smooth muscles of the digestive system.

Believed by some to be a magical plant, coca is also used in cult activities, in shamanism and divination.

---

(4) Ruggiero Romano, 1982. In Revista Allpanchis Phuturinqa, No. 19: 247

*   Museo Inka.

Botanical studies suggest that coca was native to the mountainous jungles of Peru and spread throughout the Andes; one of the oldest examples of its use was found on the northern coast of Peru at *Huaca Prieta* (2,500-1,800 BCE[5]), where *coca* leaves and containers for lime (a reactive alkaline which releases the alkaloids from the leaves) were found. In time the *Inca* State controlled the cultivation of *coca*, supplying the empire from the jungle regions near Cusco, and they also managed to acclimatize the plant and so were able to cultivate it in the Sacred Valley.[6]

Quinoa *(Chenopodium quinoa)*.   Tarwi *(Lupinus mutábilis)*.

Potato *(Solanum tuberosum)*.   Kiwicha *(Amaranthus caudatus)*.

The puma lives at higher altitudes where species such as corn, quinoa, *kiwicha, tarwi*, potatoes and other crops are cultivated.

The andean deer lives at nearly 4,000 masl. At these altitudes domestic plants are not cultivated and natural shrubs and low plants give way to grasses. These serve as forage for *guanacos, alpacas* and *llamas*, under the blue vault that limits the condor's flight.

---

(5) Lanning, 1967: 77

(6) Rev. Del Archivo Histórico del Cusco, Nro. 13: 39

MAN

Man was no stranger to this kaleidoscopic and vertiginous natural scene. Just like the fruits and seeds, he came down from the mountains following the course of the rivers through steep valleys that once seemed to be an abyss, and he reached the jungle or the sea. He also climbed, taking fruits and seeds which he acclimatized from level to level and saw them come to flower, just as the association of nature with religion flowered in his being.

Only 16000 years[7] before our era the presence of man was recorded in the caves throughout the extensive heights of the cordilleras of Peru. Jasper, obsidian, quartz and silica were the first materials that man began to transform, producing his first tools in those early workshops. Thousands of years after this first contact with stone, man would create works of singular majesty here.

In southern Peru in the area around Cusco at 3,350 masl. black, red, ochre and white were the colors that early man preferred to use to create images associated with hunting and the pasturing of the cameloids that are native to the region. He also painted images from his surroundings and used symbols whose meanings have been lost among the mountains that cradled them.

Cave paintings from high above the Sacred Valley and detail.
(at *Huayoqari*, 2,000 BCE). In the painting one can see *llamas*; a detail is reproduced.

Man, the Valley and the Altiplano

Painted, sculptured, sometimes only suggested, his traces also remain among the snowdrifts beside his extremely fragmented

---

(7) Radiocarbon gives 8000 BCE. as the date for *Lauricocha* (3,800–4,100 masl. in Huánuco) and 16000 BCE. for the site at *Pikimachay* in the southern sierra of Ayacucho.

geography. This mixed up scene is due to the meeting of two dense mountain ranges in the so-called *Vilcanota* knot. The river of the same name begins here, and streams down like a silver thread to form along its tempestuous course a rich and impressive valley, which in time the Incas would call sacred.

From the other side of the same cordillera another river rises[8] and is just barely visible as it flows across the high plains to feed Lake *Titicaca*, the highest navigable lake in the world (3,809 masl.) So, because of the same origin, or because of the water, which is at the same time a silver cord tying them together, the combined myths represent this high, wide area as the cradle of the Empire of the Sun. There the wild, rough land in all its extensive, cold and surprising solitude is covered by a mantle of pastures and dotted with thousands of black, white and multi-colored llamas and alpacas. These animals still pasture near the place where, along with tubers and grains, man once domesticated them for the first time.

Lake *Titicaca*, near the rise of the Desaguadero River.

_____

(8) This river is first known as Santa Rosa, later it becomes the *Ayaviri* and finally, at its juncture with the *Azángaro*, it becomes the Ramis and eventually empties into Lake *Titicaca*.

Similarly the day and night sky, which in these latitudes is clear and transparent during most of the year, did not escape their inquisitive look[9], and they identified the apparent movement of the sun along the horizon, the lunar periods and the stars or groups of stars that are associated in constellations (mostly those that are located along the Milky Way). Based on their observations of the rising or setting of these heavenly bodies through periodic cycles related to the sun, they were able to establish a synchronous relationship between the stars and times for planting and harvesting as well as for other activities related to their flocks.

The establishment of this synchronous connection between the Earth's natural cycles and human activities that are common to pasturing and agricultural peoples was later systematized into primitive calendars. Those who managed this were descendants of the first magicians or those who had preserved traditions that were later accumulated in "centers" associated with a landmark, and communities cnerged under their influence. Oracles and ceremonial centers sprouted up in the misty dawn on the altiplano of *Collao*. (today this territory is shared by Peru and Bolivia).

The Lake, the Guardian Spirits and the First Ages

Light blue on the clearest days, gray in cloudy or stormy moments, at 8,380 Km^2 the lake seems a living mirror of water which moderates the frigid climate of this broad extension of agricultural and pastural land. The prodigious lake, *Titicaca*, enjoyed the prestige of figuring in ancient mythologies as the origin of the world. Its beneficial nature provided abundant fish to those early men and they took realistic motifs from its rich fauna. These they identified, modified and stylized in order to perpetuated them in images which are still to be seen among the remains in their millennial settlements.

---

(9) Marshack, shows that since the rise of *Homo sapiens sapiens*, some forty thousand years ago, humans have directed their attention to the measurement of periods of time, as manifested by the movements of celestial bodies. They do this in ways that are as active, persistent and ample as the attention paid to obtaining food or making tools.
Marshack, 1972. In Sullivan, 1999: 24

Not far from the lake, in the cradle of shepherds, the *Pucara* culture (100 BCE – 100 CE) left, among other legacies, constructions whose form and contents mirrored the spirit which, stretching out its hand, taught and encouraged the people.

The Ceremonial Center of *Pucara*. It is protected by a mountain which oral tradition currently identifies with the form of a puma.

The puma (*Felix concolor*) is a carnivorous mammal that ranges over nearly all the vast geography of the Americas. In Peru it wanders in search of plunder and is now less frequently seen in coastal areas, while its tracks may also be found near livestock ranches above 4,500 masl. Or down in the jungles of the cloud forest.

With short reddish-yellow fur and the habits of a nocturnal hunter it measures more than a meter in length; it may travel many kilometers in search of its prey, but despite its fierceness it does not attack man, even when sorely pressed by hunger. Its image (with occasional changes and metamorphosis) is often found associated with cult objects used to worship water and earth; even today in popular tales from the Sacred Valley the puma is assigned the role of guardian or caretaker and is said to be a spirit that can hear people's secrets by listening through the earth.[10]

Puma cub in relief
(Detail from a monolith at *Pucara*).

Person with feline features (*Pucara*).

Puma in the shape of a fish.*

(10) Martinez and Martinez.

*   Museo Pucara.

Much closer to the lake, at *Tiahuanaco* (200 BCE– 1,000 CE), a society of herders and farmers, the flower of those ancient times, also stamped the image of the totem on what are now the remains of a famous sanctuary.

Aerial view of *Tiahuanaco*; the white line marks the pre-colombian city CIAT.[11]
Note the profile of the head of a guanaco and how the pyramid of *Akapana* serves as the animal's eye (Photo: Instituto Geográfico Militar de Bolivia).

Tiahuanaco: Temple of *Kalasasaya*.

_____

(11) Ponce, 1969: a

With complex buildings and a technology that included the knowledge of bronze metalwork, this ceremonial center became the most important cultural focal point in southern Peru; its influence extended toward the cold mountainous lands of the sierra and to the sandy desert coast. Tribute from these lands was sent to this sanctuary honoring the principal orderer of the world, *Wiracocha*, who was seen as a being with hair radiating out from his head. He carried elegantly decorated staffs and governed the world through astronomers and priests with elongated and pointed heads.[12]

Tiahuanaco: Gate of the Sun.

Detail: *Wiracocha*.

The cult of *Wiracocha* expanded (800-900 CE), this time far from Lake *Titicaca* and close to where corn flourished; his face appeared again among the artistic expressions of the sacred pottery found in the geometric cities of what was then the *Wari* state.[13] One of these cities (*Pikillacta*) was built in the pass that controlled the access to two rich corn-producing valleys: the Cusco valley and another which would later be known as the Sacred Valley of the Incas.

(12) As part of an ancient tradition some peoples who lived in what is now Peru practiced cranial deformation, a technique of binding the heads of young children to make the skull higher and narrower; "The skulls of the people from Tiahuanaco were deformed, this seemed to fulfill a function that was purely aesthetic or part of a cult." Lumbreras, 1969: 218

Ceremonial *Wari* vessel*: *Wiracocha* shines as part of the decoration, along with ears of corn.

(13) The height of the *Tiahuanaco* culture is thought to have been contemporary with the *Nazca* culture. This coastal culture left its mark on more than 450 Km² of dark red gravel on the coastal desert. Here a great diversity of lines and figures were traced, probably between 300 and 800 CE (see: Reinhard 1997: 7). The purpose of these mysterious lines, according to the majority of authors, was to represent constellations, references to the rising and setting of the sun and certain stars; and sacred paths that connected man to mountain spirits in order to obtain water and fertility. The fusion of the mutual influences of *Tiahuanaco* and *Nazca* produced a cultural expression called *Wari*.

*   Museo de la Nación – Perú.

Figures and lines in the pampas of *Nazca*. Servicio Aerofotográfico Nacional, Perú.

Much has been said about the circumstances marking the decline of these ancient societies; probably nearest the mark is the hypothesis that connects these events with natural disasters that have, over thousands of years, modified these mountainous lands. And if it is true that there is only archeological evidence of these disasters, it is also interesting to note that their ashes nourished the memory and traditions of later peoples who recognized in these remains a sacred testimony to the existence of the first ages that were described in their oldest mythologies.

THE ORIGIN OF THE CITY OF CUSCO

Centuries later, not far from these lands we've been describing, Francisco Pizarro and his men penetrated to the heart of the *Inca* empire in November of 1533, they saw there a city that filled them with astonishment. Endowed with palaces, esoteric temples, overflowing storehouses and an urban center crossed by streets that were oriented to the rising or setting of the sun, the sacred city of Cusco sheltered the lineages of the Son of the Sun under the cosmic order, and in enclosures like monasteries protected the women who were chosen for perpetual service to the cult. These women also wove the highly valued textiles with which the Incas repaid loyalties and honored their divinities.

According to Pedro Sancho's account, in 1534 nearly a hundred thousand houses were distributed to surround the city in a semi circular configuration. Within resided the ancient lineages of these lands as well as the tributary lords brought here from the most distant towns controlled by this empire. Nearly one hundred ethnic groups and twenty languages, as well as *Quechua* which was universal, co-existed in this city which was legitimately considered in its time to be the center of the world. As such, it was the nerve center of a vast communication system, connected to its farthest provinces by means of many roads and messengers, agile men called "*chaski*" who, running in relays, carried information on *quipu*, the knotted cords which they used to weave and unweave their memory. Today practically nothing is known of the codes uses to read these *quipu*; recent studies focus on the complex geometric designs of their textiles (*tocapu*). What is certain is that when the *quipumayoc* (specialists who decoded these mysterious records) were consulted about the origin of the city, they answered through a body of oral literature which was like a sacred history in which the real deeds dissolved in the magical atmosphere of myth. As such, these constituted the information provided by their records and memory to the functionaries and chroniclers of the kingdom of Spain, when the *quipumayoc* explained about the first peoples who settled near the marshy bed of the ancient evaporated lake where the city of Cusco was later built. *Lares*, *Poques*, *Sahuasiras*, *Alcabisas*, among others were the names of the primitive peoples that they said had ruled in this valley before the arrival of the Incas, the Sons of the Sun. It is not known who were the first to populate this valley, except the first name *Acamama* which means "This one that contains the things, or this one who is mother."[14]

There have been many studies about who the Incas were, these studies have asked the same question from then until now, and there have also been various answers.

Tocapu.

Quipucamayoc (1613).

_____

(14) Elorrieta, 1992: 247

There are versions of this story that are based on certain documents as well as semantic studies[15] and also certain cultural characteristics that suggest migrations of some peoples who had lived in the immediate neighborhood of Lake *Titicaca*; other studies postulate an autonomous development in the Valley of Cusco, but there is much disagreement among the different investigators. What is certain is that the epic story of their origin, as they themselves conceived and reported it, is to be found synthesized in their myths[16] and in the spirit of their works.

The Myth

From among the creations that man has in common there is one especially that in the manner of a prodigious metaphor exercises the sorcery of containing the idea of the world and man in his most remote origin. So, subtly, myth, the living inspiration of the imagination, opened the doors to this infinite space which we now call culture. Religion, arts, and social forms derive from it; so do the fabulous characteristics that were always part of it in its long and sinuous journey through the memories of the people.

The mythic cycles about the origin of man, the Incas and the city of Cusco are rich in symbols, ritual gestures and supernatural feats that are associated with descriptions of the geography in which the feat occurred. In these myths the civilizing heroes and founders are generally represented as personages who are sent by the divinity in search of a place which has previously been chosen and which will be recognizable in the moment when a ritual gesture or act made by those persons is accepted by mother nature or by those beings that reside within her, and this agreement is reflected in a natural manifestation such as a rainbow, flashes of light, or a rain of fire. This will be taken as a sign of good fortune and where it occurs on this long pilgrimage, a landmark or milestone is usually left to mark the spot. Sometimes a person in the story is changed to stone.

---

(15) The *Quechua* of Cusco, contains some 33.73% of the cognate roots of *Puquina*, a language which became extinct in the mid-seventeenth century and which has been proposed as the language that was spoken in *Tiahuanaco* (see Torero 1972: 59).

(16) The popular use of the term "myth" suggests a reference to false beliefs, but the semantic use of the term does not necessarily imply this. Cultural myths serve to organize and express shared ways of conceptualizing something since their connotation is an ideological function and serves to make the shared values, attitudes and beliefs seem "natural," "normal," "obvious," "of a common feeling" and "even true". Fiske, 1982: 93-95, Fiske and Hartley, 1978: 41. In Chandler, 1988: 66

Through cultural continuity this mythic structure still lives today. It is not surprising that after a myth is related by a member of one of the traditional communities in the Sacred Valley of the Incas, a stone marker is signaled out as being a witness or a proof of the truth of the story.[17] So the *Inca* civilization not only constructed an ideal discourse that legitimized their divine origin but at the same time they continued their communion with Nature and gave their best efforts to conceive and then physically re-create, piece by piece the scene of the epic that explained their origin. We will describe this scenery in the following section and relate the story that has been synthesized from several versions collected in the sixteenth and seventeenth centuries regarding the origin of the world, the Incas, and the city of the Son of the Sun: Cusco.

The Myth of the First Man

At the beginning of time the one who gave the world the vital breath was called *Wiracocha*, and there, where all was darkness, he placed a race of giants whom he instructed to live in peace so that they might serve him and know him for all time. But his word was not heeded by those who could not contain the emotions of pride and greed. Only then, he descended on them on rapid wings causing confusion, and his rage fell unchecked like a torment and the earth and the sea swallowed some of them and others were changed to stone as witness of this awful occasion, once the flood (called "*Unu Pachacuti*" or "water that transformed the world") ceased and the waters returned to their proper level.[18]

In connection with this tradition several chroniclers from the XVI and XVII centuries related that the monoliths that can be found in *Pucara* and *Tiahuanaco* were pointed out to them by their informants as being the petrified witnesses of the existence of these first ages of man.

Monoliths of *Tiahuanaco*.

(17) The myth that tells the origin of the community of *Amaru* in the district of *Pisac* describes some stones that are today used as boundary markers. Concerning these stones the people related that the old landlord ordered a particular stone to be buried because he feared that with this "witness" the tenant farmers would reclaim their lands. Granadino, 1993: 207

(18) Story from the chronicle of Sarmiento (1572), 1960: 206-208

Wiracochan or Tunupa, the Unifier

When the rains had passed and the land was dry, *Wiracocha* determined to populate the earth once more; only then from an island in Lake *Titicaca* he raised up the firmament, the sun, the moon, and the stars, and thus, even as the sky was populated with luminous bodies, so there also appeared on earth another, known by the name of *Wiracochan* or *Tunupa*, who showed light to men. Tall, stern, and poorly dressed, he only had a bonnet like a crown on his head and a prodigious staff as a sign of his authority and he wandered like a pilgrim throughout the Andes saying: Let the nations obey. I order you all to come forth and multiply! and so some peoples came out of lakes, while others came from springs, cliffs, caves and trees to receive from him the seeds, arts, and different tongues that each nation and people would have to cultivate. He also gave them the rules of life, speaking to them gently, teaching them not to hurt or damage one another. Those who chose to rebel were changed to stone in *Tiahuanaco*, *Pucara* and *Jauja*, others like those of the town of *Cacha*.[19] ended by building him a sanctuary after being burned by a rain of fire.

Temple of *Wiracocha*.

---

(19) This town, now called San Pedro de *Racchi*, is located 125 kilometers from Cusco, quite close to the extinct volcano of *Quinsachata* and near the temple built in memory of *Wiracocha*. Cieza de León (1,553), referring to this part of the myth and to the volcanic stones found in this place, did not fail to express the surprise appropriate to the era when he said that after the rain of fire "the stones were so consumed that they themselves are witnesses of having passed through this occurrence because they are so burnt and light that they can be lifted up like cork."

Continuing along his way *Tunupa* arrived at a place which he called Cusco, and there he prophesized the arrival of the Incas[20] then he traveled to the Sacred Valley, where he was lovingly received by the lord of *Tambo* (*Apotambo*). Here he left his knowledge engraved on his staff, and his image in the memory of the people, which they later sculpted. Finally he headed towards the equator, and lost himself in the sea, walking on top of the water as if he were the whitest foam.

In time, according to the version reported by the chronicler Joan de Santa Cruz Pachacuti, the staff left by *Wiracochan* was transmuted to gold at the moment when one of the descendants of the *Tambo* lord was born. He took the name of *Manco Capac* and taking up the staff of gold, he directed his steps to the highest parts of a mountainous land where he founded the city of Cusco.

In another version of this mythic cycle, collected by Antonio de la Calancha (1638), the beginning and the end of the story are only mentioned while the pilgrimage of *Wiracochan* is described as a journey under the earth (a metaphor that indicated a displacement in time long ago and far away) until his final apparition through a "window" in the town of *Tambo* were he was finally turned to stone.

Wiracochan turned to stone in *Tambo* or *Ollantaytambo*.

Curiously the connection established in this myth between the town of *Tambo* and the city of Cusco is also made in an ancient *Inca* prayer transcribed and translated by Cristóbal de Molina in 1573:

Oh *Wiracocha*! my father, who said let there be *cuscos* and *tambos*, let these sons of yours be conquerors and despoilers, I pray to you so that they may be fortunate and these Incas, your sons, may not be beaten nor despoiled but rather let them always be conquerors since you have made them for that.

(20) Betanzos (1551), 1880: 8

So, petrified, a landmark fixed in time in the midst of a land where the oldest memory reminds us of its multi-ethnic, many-cultured and bio-diverse condition, the peoples recognized in the same hero a common benefactor, one who represented the germ of an idea that would in time become the basis for an empire.

Later, in the same geography and due to the necessities implied by the process of development of societies, the myth of the House of Dawn and the Ayar Brothers was re-created. Their destiny this time was to establish the divine lineage of the inca rulers. The word Inca is a phoneme which varied from Enqa to Inga, meaning the spirit, force or energy which sets things in ordeer to generater or produce well-being.

Between myth and history

The Twentieth century was particularly rich in studies carried out with the purpose of discovering the location of the mythical origin of the Incas. Inevitably because they were part of the old way of thinking, these studies hypothesized the existence of the concrete concept of the myth of *Pacaritanpu*[21], the House of the Dawn, a site held to be a famous shrine from which (after having been created at Lake *Titicaca*) tradition said the first Incas emerged as gods. Nevertheless despite the numerous and dissimilar versions that exist concerning the location of this famous sanctuary, the investigators focused their studies primarily in the geographical area encompassing the Cusco province of *Paruro*, because there is a town called *Pacarectambo* (the name associated with the origin place of the Incas). Based on the chronicle of Sarmiento (1572) and on the many place names which are included in his report (some of which can be identified in the area), they thought they had resolved the mystery.[22]

---

(21) This word is often mentioned but at the time there was no standardized spelling and it was written by the chroniclers in different ways, so we have: *Pacaritanpu, Pacaritambo, Pacarictanpu, Pacarectanpu, Pacarectambo*; of these we believe that "Pacaritanpu" is the best transcription.
Pacariui: The great place where one was born (Bertonio, 1612, II: 1879: 241).
Paccarin: Dawn (Gonzales Holguin 1608, 1989: 266).
Tanpu: Lodging (Ibid).

Pacaritanpu then is understood as the lodging place of the dawn, the inn where one was born and which metaphorically means the place that witnessed the beginning of a new day, or the birth of a dynasty.

(22) Pardo, 1946; Urton, 1989; Bauer, 1992; Angles, 1995

Only later would they find out that until 1571 -one year before Sarmiento's history was finished- the town that is now called *Pacarectambo* did not even exist.[23]

This brings up a few questions. What induced the *quipumayoc* -Sarmiento names forty-two of them- to swear the truth of this part of their story? Was it perhaps that this was the final and astute act with which they protected their most precious sanctuary from destruction?

It would seem to have been so, until more than a hundred years after the arrival of the first Spanish in Cusco, when the empire no longer existed and the political and religious sway of its origin myth had dissipated. Then Bernabe Cobo (1653), an illustrious priest of that period, again investigated the memory of the first ages, and heard the story from don *Alonso Topa Atau*, grandson of the *Inca Huayna Capac*, in a version which no longer gave only an uncertain direction of the compass to locate the famous House of the Dawn. He made reference to its precise location in *Tambo*, known also as *Ollantaytambo*, a town located in the middle part of the Sacred Valley of the Incas; one of its upper stretches was known in the colonial period as the Valley of *Yucay*.

From this version, which Cobo later published in his "History of the New World", we quote several paragraphs:

"After they were placed (the Incas) by their father the sun in the lake of Titicaca, he ordered that they should take the road and the route that pleased them... And the sun their father having thus bid them goodbye, they walked to Cuzco, trying to thrust into the earth the golden staff to see where it would will them to stop, and arriving at the valley of Yucay and going a way further along the banks of the river that flows through it, they made a halt at Pacarictanpu (this means sleep that dawns)... so they came out of a cave that is at the above-mentioned seat of Tanpu, Tambo, called Pacarictanpu because of a window of stone... they came out of there when the sun came up; for this reason they gave that name to that place, setting out toward the valley of Cuzco..."

Contrary to what was thought at the time, the chronicle that was written much later by Cobo (and for that reason was scorned

---

(23) Urton, 1989. In Revista Andina, no. 1

by some investigators) contained the loose end that led the authors to explore the route that was described in this chronicle, and by comparing it with all the others that referred to the topic, it was possible to identify in the town of *Tambo* or *Ollantaytambo* not only those features and sacred landmarks that are associated with the myth, but also the famous "House of Dawn," a structure whose architecture and special orientation with respect to the sun finally made it possible to understand the apparently fantastic images discounted by earlier investigators. It seems that the images found in different stories about the origin of the Incas were also contributors to the astronomical science that permitted this civilization to integrate itself fully and harmoniously with the difficult Nature that cradled it. So they were not fantasizing in 1542 (the earliest report on this subject) when the *quipucamayoc* who was explaining about the origin of the Incas declared to the Spanish functionary, Vaca de Castro:

"...that *Manco Capac*, first *Inca*, was the Son of the Sun and came out of a window of a house and was engendered by a ray, the splendor of the sun... then he went to the heights of a mountain where the valley of Cusco can be seen..." and later founded the city.

Let us immerse ourselves in the magical setting of this story.

The Myth of the House of Dawn, the Ayar Brothers and the Founding of Cusco

Once the world was ordered, *Wiracocha* appeared in the form of a splendid man and created the Incas; then from among them he called the oldest whom he named *Manco Capac* and said to him: "You and your descendants will be great lords and will subject many nations, you will worship me as a father and you will always be respected as my children." And entrusting them with the *Tupayauri* as an insignia (this was an instrument in the fashion of a staff of gold) he told them that it was his will that they found a great city where the staff should sink into the soil.

And leaving Lake *Titicaca* behind they walked northward trying to thrust the staff of gold into the earth until they trod upon the splendid valley of *Yucay* (today known as the Sacred Valley of the Incas) and following the banks of the river that flows through it (*Willcamayu*, or

Sacred River) they arrived at *Tambo*.[24] There they entered the deep basements of the *Pacaritanpu*, which means "House of Dawn or House of Windows."[25]

In time the earth opened in the *Tanputtoco* or *Capacttoco*[26] (which is a construction in the fashion of a window directed into the earth), and, emerging from this window, *Manco Capac* was engendered by a ray of light from the sun.[27]

The pyramidal structure of the *Pacaritanpu*, located in the town of *Tambo* or *Ollantaytambo*. Note how a ray of light enters one of the "windows" (lower right corner) as it does in the myth; this umbilical cord unites the cosmos and man while the rest of the Valley remains in dark shadow. This effect is seen on the winter solstice (21st of June), the day when the festival of *Inti Raymi* –The Festival of the Sun– is celebrated.

(24) Cobo (1653), 1956 III: 147
(25) Cabello (1586), 1,951: 260-264
(26) *Tanputtoco*: The window of Tambo / *Capacttoco*: The window of the king. Betanzos (1551), 1880: 10
(27) Vaca de Castro (1542), 1929: 6-12

Detail of one of the "windows" of *Pacaritanpu* and the approximation of the effect of light that confers a sacred nature upon this site. The sun's light entering this space symbolizes the union between the Sky and the Earth, and the "illumination" of its heroes is a product of this communion, which is why they were called Sons of the Sun.

From out of this place also came *Ayar Uchu, Auca* and *Cachi* accompanied by *Mama Ocllo, Cura, Ragua,* and *Huaco,* the women who carried corn seeds and the golden vessels with which they would attend the brothers; while they, armed with halberds of gold and slings of braided sinews, climbed upwards turning around in all directions so that the light of the sun reflected on the little golden mirrors that decorated their rich outfits.

Seeing themselves strong and wise they again took up their march, only then did they notice the strength of *Ayar Cachi* because with a single shot from his sling he split a mountain (see photo, next page) and with other shots he made the mountains fall down into the valley causing much damage to Nature, so that *Manco Capac* or *Ayar Manco,* who was the most prudent, agreed with the idea his brothers had to separate *Ayar Cachi* from them, and to manage this they said, "Brother, we know that we have left behind in the *Capacttoco* the golden drinking vessels and the *Napa*[28] which is our most important insignia; it would be best for everyone if you would go bring them to us."

---

(28) The *Napa* was a white alpaca covered by red mantle and with golden earrings which the rich Incas carried to symbolize their abundant flocks. Sarmiento, 1572/1960: 215

Views of a curious geological formation with a stone wedged in the middle. Oral tradition in *Ollantaytambo* says this was the work of *Ayar Cachi's* slingshot.

So, sweetly, they begged him to go back into the place whence they had emerged and there he finally remained buried. On that day the earth shook.

After weeping for his death they agreed with the people of the surrounding area to set up a village that they called *Tanpuquiro* which means "lodgings like teeth," and they forgot about him. But one day they saw him return, held up on enormous wings of colorful feathers. They were afraid and wanted to flee but he soon took that fear from them saying: "Do not be afraid and do not grieve because I have only come to tell you that now it is time to begin to know the power that our father gave us; I ask you to leave this valley and continue until you encounter the place where you will build a sumptuous temple to worship the Sun. I will pray to *Wiracocha* that in a short while you will become lords and I will remain on a hill that is near here"; despite this he was knocked down by a shot from a sling and with a broken wing he remained there, finally turned to stone.[29]

---

(29) Cieza de León (1553), 1880: 20

Monument of stone that in the manner of a sacred landmark recreates this part of the myth. It is found in *Ollantaytambo* and represents the image of a condor. In this complex there are also numerous carved altars to be found.

Artist's rendition of the monument dedicated to *Ayar Cachi*.

In the Andean cosmogony these conversions to stone, which is to say the passage from one form of life to another, does not imply a definite separation from this world, but rather it is assumed that from their new state those beings continue to contribute to the dynamic process of life. That is why this monumental sculpture, as well as having singular characteristics of aesthetic expression, was conceived so that it not only shows us the natural expression of its form but also the context which recreates the time when, according to their religious ideas, all of Nature was regenerated.

The winter solstice in the Andes marked the time when the sun was reborn and the world revitalized, and the summer solstice marked the time of coming to naturity. The characteristics which the images of the sun has in the drawings of Guaman Poma (1613) show these ancient concepts.

And so since the sun was thought to be reborn on June 21st the other divinities were likewise reborn. Note in the photo that during the first hours of the morning the part that corresponds to the head of this monument projects a shadow which is the allegory of his spirit newly appearing in the world.

Six months later during the summer solstice (December 22nd, when the Nature has ripened and matured), his "vitality" descended over the earth at midday to receive the offerings placed on his altar. According to the ancient tradition at this time of the year when *Capac Raymi*, or the Great Feast is celebrated, the dead return to communicate with the living. The Incas held fiestas with their ancestors. According to Cobo (1653), "The reason that they took out the bodies of the dead was so that their descendents could drink with them as if they were still alive and on this occasion they ask their ancestors to make them as brave as they once were."

Note in this photographic sequence how the shadow created
by the part that corresponds to the beak in the representation of this bird
descends toward the altar which is destined to serve him food, and it is positioned
so that a shadow is cast right in the middle of the altar, where there is a
gnomon that allows the date of the summer solstice to be fixed.

After this transformation into stone the brothers called together ten *Ayllu* (communal groups) and set off with them to search for the place that had been described to them. Leading the cortege *Manco Capac* carried the staff of gold in one hand and in the other hand he carried the sacred bird, Indi, protected in a basket; they say that he exercised a strange power over those who followed him.

Manco Capac and the bird Indi. Drawing by Antonio de Herrera (1615).

Not being satisfied by the lands that they found, they returned to *Tanpuquiro* where *Mama Ocllo*, wife of *Manco Capac*, gave birth to a son who they called *Sinchi Roca*. After the feast days celebrating his birth they again took up the march which this time lead them to the foot of a mountain that they called *Huanacauri*. Here they determined their destiny: *Manco Capac*, who already had a son, was to be their leader, *Ayar Uchu* would remain there like a sacred stone (*Huaca*) and *Ayar Auca* from wherever they ordered would take the land that they had to populate. This decided, they turned their eyes to the top of the mountain we have mentioned and they saw a rainbow which they took as a sign that the world would never again be destroyed by water; but the fate of *Ayar Uchu* was already cast, since he turned to stone right in the place where the rainbow was born. Later, advancing toward the peak a bit more, they tried to thrust the golden staff into the earth and finally it sank in. It was from this very spot that *Manco Capac* saw a promontory that ran down into the swampland at the head of an enormous valley and, showing it to his brother *Ayar Auca*, he said to him: "look at that rock and go flying over there (because they say that he had sprouted wings) and when you seat yourself there you will take possession of that place." Upon hearing these words he did as he was ordered and finally he turned to stone right there, as a landmark showing possession, which in the language of this valley was called Cusco.[30] Garcilaso de la Vega (1609) gives for the name of Cusco a symbolic meaning that is very similar, and says that Cusco, which comes from the *Quechua* word "*Qosqo*" means navel of the world.

---

(30) Sarmiento (1572), 1960: 213-218

The Ceremonial Center called Inticancha is born

It was beginning with this myth that the *quipucamayoc* registered the occurences that they divined in time and told centuries later, the deeds of the *Inca* lineage. Among these they recounted how at the dawn of this civilization the Son of the Sun appeared in the valley of Cusco shining with the light of the Sun in his golden clothes and together with the crowd that followed that image, he took the high ground situated between the marshland fed by two rivers (*Saphy* and *Tullumayu*). There *Manco Capac* founded the *Inticancha* or House of the Sun, but before he could do that, *Mama Ocllo*, his wife and an indomitable warrior, threw out the people who had ruled there.

So a ceremonial center was born at 3,350 masl. in a dry, healthy valley surrounded by a sea of mountains, and at that moment the heart began beating of something that one day would become the Empire of the Four Corners of the World: *Tahuantinsuyo*. Later they would mark off four spaces called *cancha* or courtyards around the temple they had built to treasure the stone that had once been *Ayar Auca*, and starting there they began to take over the rest of the valley so that they might worship the Sun and see their cornfields flower.

The city of Cusco. On the ashes and foundations of what were once
the principal temples of the capital of the Inca empire today the lovely,
slender colonial temples stand proudly.

It was not long before some of the people already living in the surrounding valley began to send tribute to the temple and *Manco Capac*, seeing himself grow old, ordered the ten *ayllu* that had accompanied him from the House of Dawn on his epic journey to promise to be the guarantors and protectors of his lineage; he finally gave the power to his son *Sinchi Roca*, and to his lineage he left his "*huauque*" or "double" to be an oracle which would be worshiped in the image of the bird *Indi*.

In the version transcribed by Sarmiento (1572) the Incas who followed consolidated their hold over the Cusco valley until the reign of *Inca Roca*, the sixth in the dynasty, when the Sons of the Sun stopped living in the temple compound and set up their residence nearby. Perhaps we could say this was the end of the period marked by the ceremonial center and a city was finally born; in the future (and after the Incas overcame the siege of warriors who arrived from out of the depths of the *Apurimac* gorge) this city would flower under the aegis of *Inca Yupanqui*.

Ruins of the monument said to have been the residence of *Inca Roca*.

Pachacutec, Inca Yupanqui

Described as a noble man whose destiny apparently was to have kept him far from power, *Inca Yupanqui* turned this around when he defended the sacred city of Cusco from the invading *Chanca* warriors. The city was undefended because it had been abandoned by both his terrified father, *Inca Wiracocha*, and the official successor, *Inca Urco*. Victorious at the end and going against tradition, *Inca Yupanqui* was crowned with the imperial tassel and acclaimed by the people with the name of *Pachacutec* (He who transforms the world). A skillful politician, wise in that he well knew the cloth woven by the interests of the ancient lineages who disputed his power, he made a pilgrimage to the House of Dawn, instituting it as an oracle and a universal shrine. So, after reforming the calendar and taking the town of *Tambo* for his own, he was able to subdue and control those who questioned the legitimacy of his government[31].

In time he constructed a government with a pyramidal court, with the *Inca* at the top, supported by the class of noble blood, below them the class of privilege and then the common people. He administered the resources of the realm through a system of accounting by tens: the head of each family reported to one man who controlled ten, and he reported to one higher up who also was responsible for ten, and so forth up to the one who controlled forty thousand. After organizing this system of government, he began the reconstruction of Cusco, which through his disposition and design ceased being a city of mud and straw and took stone as the material that was used to cement and construct the edifices that would consolidate his image and his rule. For twenty years more that fifty thousand men worked without rest building aqueducts, storehouses, temples, palaces and whatever else the city needed, a city that little by little took on the shape of its totem animal: the Puma.

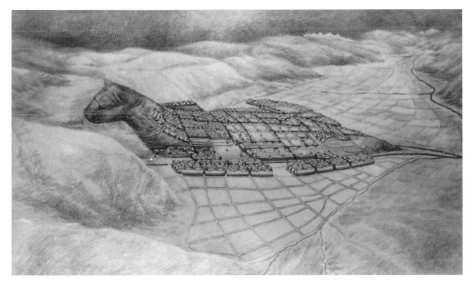

Artist's rendering of Cusco, the Puma city.

(31) Sarmiento (1572), 1960: 237-239

35

From the heart of this city, the central plaza, to the four corners of the world he also directed the roads that he and his army used to take the high lands, establishing resting places at the end of each day's march, and he kept these rest stops, called *tambo*, well provisioned. There they supplied themselves with salt, potatos, quinoa, and llamas with which they descended to the edge of the jungle to return loaded with coca, gold, food and colored feathers.

String of llama. and road descending to the jungle.(*Wiñayhuayna*).

Some of the many roads, which during the height of the empire created an inter-connected net of more than 23,000 kilometers,[32] ran along the edges of deep chasms in the mountainous terrain or chanced them by crossing

The bases of an Inca bridge that crossed the *Vilcanota* River at *Ollantaytambo*, and the *Queswachaca* bridge over the *Apurimac* River.

(32) Hyslop, 1992: 54-56

hanging bridges suspended between sharp rocks to enter the widely scattered inter-andean valleys and the valleys of the coastal desert. Corn, beans, garlic, cotton, peanuts, dried fish, and seashells were among the products that flowed into the sacred city as tribute, and they brought fine sand from the seashore, to spread in the plaza where all these roads met.

The governors of the subject peoples and the flower of their provinces were brought from *Pasto* (Colombia), and the *Bio Bio* River in the extreme southern part of the empire (Chile). Potters, metal workers, weavers, skilled craftsmen, and the gods they worshiped were brought to Cusco so that, on walking through the city, according to Garcilaso (1609), "one could see and understand the whole empire as if looking into a mirror or a cosmographic painting", while the spirit of the empire was materialized at the Temple of the Sun, called *Qoricancha*.

THE QORICANCHA

Built on the same site where the ancestors had constructed their first temple, the *Qoricancha* (Gold Courtyard) represented for the empire the golden mirror in which the Andean peoples, reverent and barefoot, saw themselves.

Supplied with all that could be created, this reflection was the desire of Inca *Pachacutec* after receiving a crystal mirror in a dream (even before he conquered his enemies and was crowned); in this sheet of crystal, splendid as the sun, Wiracocha showed him all that which would someday be his vast empire.[33]

The Qoricancha was built as a display of the finest and most harmonious architecture; the oldest parts are constructed of green diorite, they used red andesite in the gardens and dark gray andesite for the compound walls and the temple rooms; these rooms had niches and trapeziodal[34] doorways and were dedicated to the Sun, the Moon, the stars, Lightning and the Rainbow. These enclosures were collected in a single complex around a large central courtyard with a fountain in the center. Beyond the esoteric meaning of the colors and the riches it contained, now lost to us, this architecture reflected the solidity inspired by the surrounding andean countryside as well as the austere and balanced nature of its builders.

---

(33) Molina (1574), 1943: 20

(34) The function of the trapezoidal design is quite similar to that of the arch, where the force is divided laterally and vertically; the trapezoid became the signature form of Inca architecture.

The cloister of the Santo Domingo convent was built on top of the enclosures located around the fountain and the broad patio of the *Qoricancha*.

After the devastating earthquake which shook Cusco in 1950 and destroyed part of the cloister, the restorers freed the enclosures of the unharmed *Qoricancha* from the ruins of the colonial buildings that had been superimposed upon them. The enclosures dedicated to Lightning and the Rainbow are visible in the photograph.

The enclosure of the Stars.

Detail of the interiors.

Since that time (after the temple that represented the center of the empire was completed) the cult of *Wiracocha* flowered and even though the *Inca* religion might be understood to be polytheist, in reality it was monotheist since those elements understood as multiple divinities (the Sun, the Moon, the stars, the earth and its elements, the civilizing heroes and even the mummies of the ancestors) were only seen as intermediaries of the supreme being, the invisible substance adored by the initiates, the priests, and the wise men who lived in this temple. The ancient *Inca* prayers that were transcribed in 1613 by the native chronicler Joan de Santa Cruz Pachacuti seem to say so.

Prayer to *Wiracocha*

Oh Wiracocha!
supreme foundation
lord who says:
let this man be,
let this woman be.
Lord of light and of generation,
Where are you?
May I not see you?
Is your royal altar
in the upper world?
in the lower world?
on the Earth?
Hear me
You! who in the sea above
remains
and in the sea below
is changed,
Animator of the Universe
creator of human beings
Lord of lords

I wish to look
at you
with my imperfect eyes.
Then seeing you,
knowing you,
understanding you,
you will see me
and you will know me.
The sun and the moon,
the day and the night,
the summer and the winter,
not in vain
do they go to the place that is chosen
and they arrive at their limit.
Whatever may be the scepter
which you have made me take up
Hear me
listen to me
while I am still not tired
or dead.[35]

---

(35) Inca prayer written down by the native chronicler, Joan de Santa Cruz Pachacuti (1613), 1927: 148

It is known that for these noblemen, who were distinguished from common men by having their head shaved[36] and the lobes of their ears stretched by heavy pendants, gold signified more than something valuable for exchange; because of its color and incorruptibility the metal was associated with the cult of the solar spirit, who knew its splendor in the *Qoricancha*.

Inca idol, with deformed earlobes.*

Documents from the sixteenth century describe the Temple of the Sun as being crowned by a border or edging of gold and in its interior, where the sacred fire was permanently tended, the sheets of gold that hung on the walls gilded a scene in which, thanks to an ingenious artifice, a disk burnished with the figure of the sun reflected the first rays and lit up this room and especially the human figure of the idol *Punchao* (which means day). In the belly of this figure there was a repository which held the ashes of the hearts of their *Inca* ancestors.[37]

Inca praying at the House of Dawn. Note the shaved head and enormous ears.
Guaman Poma 1613.

---

(36) Today popular illustrations depict the Inca leaders with long hair since after the Spanish style was imposed in the sixteenth century, the noblemen adopted it. This image was later spread through idealized pictures of the Incas from the past. But the documents that describe them suggest the opposite, this is the case with Garcilaso's description and the drawings of Guaman Poma.

(37) Cobo (1653) 1956 III: 360-361. This idol, described forty years after the arrival of the first Spanish in Cusco, was finally captured along with *Felipe Tupac Amaru* when the rebellion in his redoubt in *Vilcabamba* was quashed.

*   Museo Inka.

They also described how in the most important part of the temple, invisible and hidden in the most inaccessible and profound depths of his essence, The *Wiracocha* Universe was interpreted by Santa Cruz Pachacuti. And later drew in a diagram with the principal elements of the *Inca* Religión.

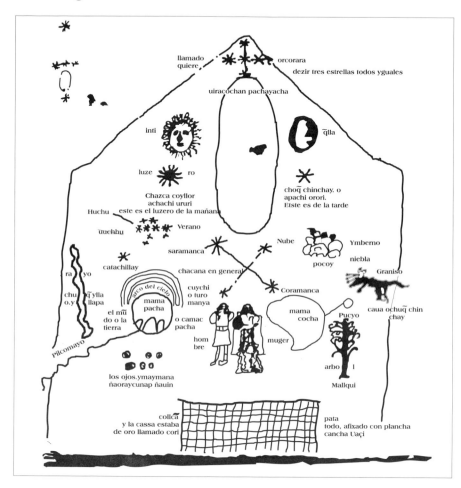

And so, even as once in this same place *Ayar Auca* had turned to stone on the spot and this landmark registered the possession of the Cusco Valley, when the temple was finished *Inca Pachacutec* ordered the mummies of past Incas to be dug up (they represented the germinating seeds and the living trunk of the common tree of the imperial lineages), so that then they could be placed in seats of gold. From there, still classed as sacred and therefore, within the terms of symbolism and tradition treated as if they were alive, they claimed for him the rights of full power.

Artist's recreation of the *Qoricancha*.

Of the buildings of the temple of the sun nothing remains today since the church of Santo Domingo was built upon this spot.

The church of Santo Domingo.

Contemporary studies have determined that at the beginning of the fifteenth century
the constellation of the Pleiades was aligned with the magnificently worked corridor
that can be seen in the photograph.

Silver, plentiful and finely laminated, was dedicated to the enclosure of the moon (today partially destroyed). The moon was venerated in the image of a woman. Stars were worshiped in the building beside it and representations of the stars hung from the roof like those that shone in the sky,[38] since the Incas believed that all beings on earth had their likeness in the stars and that man's sustenance depended upon their favor. It is also known that cultivating their ancient traditions they recognized the planets, among them Venus which was called *Chaska* (star with long hair), Jupiter (the granary), Mars (ember of fire) and stars or groups of stars that were grouped into constellations; recent studies established an astronomical orientation aligning one side of this complex with the constellation that protected corn plants (the Pleiades,)[39] and even today right around the *Qoricancha* a simple curious look allows us to see that on the summer solstice the sun lines up with one of the side streets.

In this temple which is located where the weather is dry for half the year, Lightning, Thunder and the Rainbow were also venerated in their own enclosures as the forces that herald the invaluable rain that fertilizes the soil and supplies the flow to the fountains of this fantastic garden. Here they placed golden, life-sized figures of men, plants and animals and all else they could offer to Mother Earth on pedestals, because, according to tradition, whatever is given, that same will be received in equal portion.

Clearly since this information comes through the chroniclers from secondary sources these reports might easily be taken as imaginary if it were not that many of the pieces that were described (among them the sheets of gold from the temple walls) were parceled out in the division of the treasure as reported by Francisco Pizarro in 1533.

There is also written testimony describing how, from inside the nucleus of the *Qoricancha* and radiating through the barrier of its walls, forty-one imaginary lines extended outwards. These not only gave structure to the social organization of the imperial lineages but above all served to connect more than three hundred shrines that were located at distances of up to ten kilometers in all directions around the city. Among the shrines were astronomical observatories. Reciprocally the

(38) Garcilaso (1609), new edition undated: 184

(39) Zuidema, 1983: 151

information collected by these observatories converged at the temple, and the temple oracle predicted the climate and weather conditions for the year and defined the relation of time and the use of space in its dominions.

So the dynasty of lower Cusco had its nucleus in this place where the gods of conquered peoples, the forces of nature, the men who had become timeless mummies and the most ancient traditions all converged.

Complementing the infrastructure that consolidated the image of power and richness of the city, the House of the Chosen Women was built nearby. These women were dedicated to making sure the needs of the temple were permanently supplied; as well as preparing the ritual food and drink, and weaving a massive amount of fine textiles which were used in the empire to distinguish between the different social levels and were an important part of an economy based on redistribution.

Loreto street: On the right we see part of the wall that surrounded the House of the Chosen Women (*Acllahuasi*).

To the north of the *Qoricancha*, up on top of the hill that overlooks the city, the dynasty of upper Cusco that had been founded by *Inca Pachacutec* built for itself the finest of all the temples in the empire, a construction which, in the context of the sacred concept of the city, represented the head of the spirit-puma, which the city embodied.

SACSAYHUAMAN

There are few chroniclers who mention its form when discussing the characteristics of the city of Cusco; among the most notable is Juan de Betanzos (1551) who attributed to *Pachacutec* the idea of associating the City and its surroundings with the body and limbs of a puma; and Sarmiento (1572) names *Pachacutec* as the designer and *Tupac Inca Yupanqui*, his son, as the one who organized the construction of this megalithic head, known ever since then as *Sacsayhuaman*, which in the ancient language of the city means festooned-head.[40]

Thousands of men working for over fifty years supplied the force that the *Inca* state required as tribute. They extracted enormous blocks of limestone from nearby quarries (it has been calculated that some of these weigh more than one hundred tons). After being roughly shaped, they were transported on wooden rollers[41] and inclined planes to the site where, once they were completely shaped and finished, they were joined to build these impressive walls.

---

(40) *Sacsa*: Festooned   *Uma*: Head

(41) Studies carried out by Thor Heyerdahl (1959) on Easter Island estimate that fifteen men were needed to drag one ton across the ground. Tests made in *Ollantaytambo* (INC) gave similar results.

Variously identified as a fortress, the House of Weapons and War, and also as a Temple for prayer and sacrifice, this monument was built above the city on top of a mountain where tradition says the guardian spirits lived. It was built to show in a visible form the sign that represented the head of the Empire or the fount of superhuman power.

This then explains the reason for its construction and the fact that *Sacsayhuaman* may be one of the few human constructions that by its presence alone is able to arouse the sensations of astonishment and perplexity that are usually the immediate response to this enormous structure, and it does this without ceasing to be part of the natural surroundings from which it emerges.

This integration, profound and harmonious, which connected the countryside (which at that time was considered sacred) with man's work made *Inca* architecture famous and the finest of their temples was a colossal altar to the Nature and man's religious spirit.

Sacsayhuaman and the city of Cusco.

The so-called throne of the Inca, cut from living rock.

Reports from the sixteenth century were unable to escape the aura generated by *Sacsayhuaman* and, marveling at its construction, those who knew it while it was still intact described it among other sites.

If it was the pen of Martin de Murua (1590) which showed it naked, "(Sacsayhuaman) seems to be the work of giants or a wall that is more of nature than of art," it was Garcilaso (1609) who defined the political function of this type of architecture: "the best work which the Incas ordered to be made to show their power and majesty was the fortress of Cusco whose greatness cannot be believed by one who has not seen it, and he who has seen it and looked at it carefully begins to imagine and still believes that these deeds were done with enchantment or that those who built it were demons and not men..."

Endowed with three impressive, successive and ascending bulwarks in zig-zag form that represent the wrinkled head of a puma and crown the top of the mountain below which stretches its invisible body (comprised of the old part of the city of Cusco), this monument was also said to have a secret source of water and numerous rooms, among them storehouses filled with food, textiles, metals, and arms, while in the highest part there were three towers; the largest of which was circular with four stories. Its foundations are still visible today.

Foundation of the tower of *Muyucmarca*.

One can also appreciate the artistic cut of cyclopean, polygonal blocks, which fit together plastically and suggest to us an unknown and mutilated language[42] which today remains beside all that is left of *Sacsayhuaman*. The destruction of the towers and buildings began in 1537, and by 1559 they had been completely dismantled and the blocks limestone used to build the cathedral in the plaza of Cusco.

In the surrounding area are terraces, cemeteries, shrines, ritual fonts, subterranean passageways and astronomical observatories as witnesses to the past, and they were written in the pages of history when they were taken and used by *Manco Inca* in the rebellion of 1536.

(42) Studies in the general theory of the symbology of walls were begun by Maik del Solar.

Although *Inca* architecture gives us the impression of uniformity of design because of its characteristic style, for the attentive observer it is easy to see that each one of their complex creations is different from the rest (in the form and placement of the blocks that structured the monuments and in the context in which they were placed); it is as if each monument avoided repeating patterns and sought to create through the manifestations of its forms the necessary spaces to submerge us in the atmosphere of the site where it was built.

Thus for example in the *Qoricancha* the severity of the symmetrical lines, the perfection translated through the polish and beautiful finish of its geometric and sloping walls, and the harmonious proportions of the rows of blocks that are smaller in size as they crown each one of the solid enclosures and the exterior wall, gives us the sensation of a perfect order where it was believed that the divine, ethereal entity to whom the temple was dedicated resided. These artists who had this vision of celestial beauty also directed the construction of complex buildings in which earthly beauty is reflected in the images of the spirits of the Nature which reside, in a subtle and interior fashion, in individual blocks, and show themselves in hieratic faces during different periods of the year when the light of the sun falls on the relief, or on that rare kind of mosaic that is created by the polygonal blocks at *Sacsayhuaman*. These, which because of their level of abstraction are in themselves sculptures, become architecture in the measure that each one of them fits harmoniously with the others around it, because for the *Inca* sense of eternity the embellishment of the wall (because of its stable and durable character) had in itself an environmental value. It is because of this that the figures structured in them, which also represented images of the spirits who propitiate life and fertility, escaped from being merely decorative and lay hidden so that they do not detract from the marvelous whole achieved by the textures, relief and forms of each one of the polygons that make up these exquisite complexes.

Today it is known that each one of these blocks was shaped using hammers of bronze and very hard stones (hematite and quartzite) and were polished with granite sand, plenty of water, clay and plants until their forms and edges fit exactly with the copies or clay molds that had been taken from the blocks that were just above and below them.

Many of the blocks used to construct the walls of *Sacsayhuaman* were designed in such a way that once they were joined together they gave the impression of figures representing people animals and plants. The groupings of these figures in and of themselves could also have meaning (These photos have been digitally done to highlight the figures found in the walls).

In these images one can make out the figures of a fish and a bird.

Four enormous doors on the first level, five on the second (two of which can be seen in the photographs on this page) and five more on the third level invite one to enter and wander through the spaces in this massive monument.

Nowadays the invocation of *Inti Raymi* or festival of the Sun is held on the broad field at *Sacsayhuaman* as part of the festivities celebrated in the city every June, while in September the ceremony of *Warachicuy* is enacted there as well. The Festival of *Warachicuy* consisted of tests of prowess and ceremonial rites of passage which boys had to undergo in order to be initiated into manhood; now these tests are represented by choreographed gymnastics. According to Garcilaso, during one of these tests the young men had to take and then defend each level of these monumental bulwarks.

The Evocation of the festival of *Warachicuy*.

Qenqo

Nearby, among the hundreds of shrines that encircle Cusco, one finds some rocky outcrops that ancient tradition says were the continuation, or visible elements, of the inside of the Earth; among these *Qenqo* is quite noticeable because of the mysterious character conferred upon it by the hands of the master planners. Worked onto the rock is a fascinating combination of planes, forms, and improbable modulations that induces the spectator to lose himself in the secret nature of the symbols. A recurrent stair step sign leads us to them and the spaces associated with the complex show them to us.

Qenqo, mysterious Andean sanctuary.

In the stair step sign the three horizontal lines represent space and, between them, the two vertical lines represent time. The first step is related to the world in which we live and which is possible to transcend (*Kay Pacha*). The vertical line points out the time that is necessary to know the second step, or the interior world (*Ukhu Pacha*). This is the space-time in which, through dreams or dead, one  finds the passage to the exterior world and the canal through which communication is established between mankind and the divinities who inhabit *Hanan Pacha*. This is the space associated with the concept of the cosmos, Eternity, the infinite or the idea of God which is symbolized by the third step.

In this same complex in the area that corresponds to *Kay Pacha* (this world), a rock stands upright; its form and details represent a toad that receives rainwater. It sits there as a focal center and around it opens a semi-circular space like one of the small pools where these animals live, which is one of the reasons that " it (the toad) was connected in mythology to the life-giving corpuscles of springs,... and was often represented (in manifestations of art) whether it be in the middle of a fountain or around the borders."[43]

Because of the nature of its biological cycle which the farmers say usually expresses the changes and possible tendencies of the weather (that is to say because it usually hides during the dry season and reappears at the beginning of the rainy season to reproduce and spawn in the fields if the weather is normal, or in the bottom of the irrigation ditches if a drought is about to begin), the toad was also considered to be the announcer and propitiator of the rains, since in this world (Kay Pacha) where water is so scarce, most of the cultivated crops depend on regular rainfall. In 1,621 Ramos Gavilán wrote: "they are accustomed to putting idols shaped like toads up on the cliffs... believing that with this ceremony they would acquire the water that they so desire."

Today in the language of the traditional communities they call the biggest toads *Pachacuti* (turned-over world), a word that is also associated with the changes that come about through natural disasters provoked by the excess or the lack of water.

---

(43) Carrión, 1955: 14

Near the area we have been describing is an access which spans a short distance and leads to an interior passageway (*Ukhu Pacha*), which is interpreted as a transitory space. Its infrastructure, such as niches, tables and an impressive altar in the fashion of a funerary mound evokes the ceremonies of mummification and the world of the dead. The discovery of human remains at this spot during the last century seems to confirm this.

Concerning the techniques used to carry out these burial rites, studies reveal that these were done by bleeding the corpse from the femoral vein, emptying the brain matter from the skull and in many cases the body was disembowelled through a cut in the diaphragm. The bodies were placed in the fetal position. The dry climate, the cold of the night, the heat of the day and the use of plants such as molle (*Schinus molle*) and muña (*Mintostachys setosa*) allowed the bodies of those who were chosen as offerings to the mountain spirits, as well as the bodies of those who belonged to the ruling class, to remain preserved through time.

In the exterior part of the complex, the part that corresponds to Hanan Pacha, one finds two cylindrical prominences near a profusion of faceted modulations in the rock; these are oriented in relation to the apparent movement of the sun and were used to determine the changes of season. In the photograph one can see its orientation with respect to the rising sun on the day of the winter solstice.

These elements which allowed them to study and understand the cosmic phenomena in the science of astronomy were also oriented (as in all the ancient societies) so as to connect or establish relations between the stars and human lives through oracles and augury (astrology). One of these elements corresponds to a fountain associated with the form of a tadpole; the light on the sun settles on its head on the winter solstice and the zig zag canal forms its body (qenqo). When liquids were let flow through the channels, the random path they took fortold favorable or unfavorable future events for those who consulted the oracle.

Tambomachay and *Puca Pucara*

Since remote times living in a geography of extremes like the Andes has implied the need to make the best use of scarce natural resources. Among these is water, vital for survival and the development of the only civilization in the Americas that practiced major livestock ranching, raised flocks of animals and was able to achieve the domestication of numerous species and varieties of plants as a few peoples in the world have done.

Worshippers and tributaries of a religion in which all of nature was held sacred, they saw in the springs and lakes not only the base or matrix where the protective powers reside but also the origin places of lineages that were inspired by necessity and undertook daring human enterprises to build reservoirs, channels, aqueducts and water fountains in this unlikely topography because the survival of its inhabitants depended on the careful control and supply of these water systems. One can understand why some studies have not hesitated to call the ancient cultures from this part of the world hydraulic societies, societies in which power and well-being were concentrated in those who controlled the use of water and made it sacred in order to do so.

And because of this fact it is well-known that of the nearly three hundred and fifty shrines that surrounded Cusco, ninety-two of them are related to springs and water sources. Among them there is one that was called *Quinua Puquio*[44] (The Spring of the Quinoa) which today is known as *Tambomachay*; they gave this site a studied architectural stage-setting order to emphasize it as a source of underground water, as well as to reduce the chaos of appearances of the dual symbols contained in the number of its niches and founts where they carried out purification rituals.

Half a kilometer downstream, at the beginning of the trail that leads to the Sacred Valley and from there to the warm, moist lands of the subtropical forest, they built *Puca Pucara*[45]: The Red Fort. The tribute[46] of coca leaves, peppers, yucca, medicinal plants, feathers and gold coming from the lowlands was registered here at this pass that controlled the entry of men and products into the sacred city of Cusco which the chronicler Polo (1571) called the house and dwelling place of the gods, where there was no spring, nor step, nor wall that was not possessed of mystery.

Tambomachay.

Puca Pucara.

(44) See Bauer Brian, 2000: 86

(45) The original name of this place was probably *Caynaconga*, a shrine that Polo (1571) described as a rest stop for the Inca.

(46) Cieza de León (1553) 1973, in referring to one of the main entrances to the city, mentioned that in these places there were "...gatekeepers who charged for rights and tribute that they were obliged to give to the lords."

63

THE SACRED VALLEY OF THE INCAS

Pisac

At some distance from Cusco, between the skirts of lofty mountains, some with peaks that are over five thousand meters high, the *Vilcanota* River, or *Wilcamayu* (Sacred River), runs green and peaceful throughout the dry season; when the first rains come, it becomes cloudy and turbulent in its age-old task of carving out the valley. Because of the quality of its soils, the benevolent climate, the richness of its heavenly flora and fauna[47], its exceptional beauty, as well as its association with the cosmos, the valley was granted special privilege and was called sacred[48] by the Sons of the Sun. Held to be a territory that does not belong to any provinces of the *Tawantinsuyo* Empire, the Sacred Valley was the personal holding of the Inca Rulers, and was built as a direct extension of the city of Cusco.

Far below, invisible, at an average height of 2,850 masl. and blessed with a pleasant climate, the Sacred Valley of the Incas lies at the foot of this chain of mountains (here photographed after a heavy snowfall).

(47) Garcilaso (1607), undated: 108-109, commented about this: "That valley has more advantages than all the others that are in Peru, and for that reason the Inca Kings ever since Manco Capac, who was the first, right up to the last of them had it as their garden and the place of their delights and recreation... the skirts of the mountains are rich in abundant pastures and full of deer, bucks, guanacos, and vicuñas, and partridges and many other birds, although the squandering and wastefulness of the Spanish have already nearly destroyed all that was good hunting..."

(48) Garcilaso (1607): 80 defines the *Quechua* word "*huaca*" or "sacred" (one of its various accepted meanings) as all that which in excellence and beauty is superior to the rest.

In concept the area called the Sacred Valley stretches for about a hundred kilometers between *Pisac* and *Machupicchu* and includes several towns and the majority of the monuments that were built during the Empire of the Incas. Among them is *Pacaritanpu*, a sanctuary named in mythology as the place where the Sons of the Sun originated. This is one of the reasons that the cosmology of the Incas associated this valley and the river that runs through it with the *Mayu* or the River of stars which we call the Milky Way.[49]

The Sacred Valley and the Milky Way

Religious tradition established that the beings upon the Earth each had a common ancestor in the stars[50] and in the celestial vault they identified those stars which for reasons of astronomical and religious character were needed to configure constellations such as the Tree or the Condor. Taking the Milky Way as the principal frame of reference for observing the sky, they also connected some of the stars with the dark clouds scattered along its length which formed the so-called "black constellations". Among these the Llama, Toad, Fox, and Snake are recognizable.

On earth, the Inca, deified as the Son of the Sun and held to be the benefactor of men, also showed the attributes of a divided nature, and each of them, beginning with the first of the dynasty, chose for himself an idol which he identified as his brother, and which continued to be worshiped through time as if it were he himself.

Analogously, in the pastoral and agricultural communities which today are repositories of some of these beliefs, it is believed that "the forces that are beyond the Earth - God, the sun, the moon, the stars - have limited powers. Where these external forces may be absorbed (or represented on the Earth) is when they acquire power. Only then when the stars are connected with a particular peak of a mountain do they become incarnate and from there they control the destiny of man."[51]

---

(49) The Milky Way is a band of white diffuse light that crosses the heavens; it is formed of millions of stars and includes dark areas of dust and gas.

(50) Cobo (1653), 1956 III: 365

(51) Condori/Gow 1982: 7

So the Inca civilization did not escape from the common idea that led them to believe, as did many peoples around the world, in the existence of a double or a celestial archetype of the beings and places where they lived as well as the cities and temples where they worshipped them.[52] So when the descendants of the Inca nobility spoke to Cobo (1653) and told him about their common ancestors and about their earthly representations, he wrote down this version in his "History of the New World":

"They say that those first men, after having named a successor, turned into those same places, some turned to stones, others became falcons or condors and other birds and animals, and **because of this the temples and huacas that they adore have different forms and figures**."

Forms and figures re-created in the enormous ritual spaces in the Sacred Valley represented the constellations that were located in the Milky Way, the Celestial River; it was as if the valley and its river were a double or a reflection of the Milky Way in earthly space.

The river flowed from the sanctuary of *Vilcanota* where the Inca mythology believed the Sun was born,[53] and fertilized the earth, later it would join the profound depths of the sea; it is projected in the sky as a river of stars to complete the sacred cycle in which men and gods communed. Today those who follow tradition in the valley make offerings to the river in the belief that their requests will become reality when the rains begin.

The Constellations mirrored in the Sacred Valley

To make this cosmological vision concrete must have demanded considerable time and continuous effort, given the magnitude of the work, since Inca architecture was designed not only to satisfy practical requirements but also as a function of the symbols and magical nature which a must include and represent.

Magic, practiced with the object of escaping from direct causality, constituted an active component in their beliefs in the measure in which it sought to conciliate and connect the powers of nature and those of desire; for the same reason they conceived of the Universe as a living whole, its parts joined by vital and invisible ties; later this concept was synthesized in their architecture through their works.

To achieve this aim they took advantage of natural formations already present in the mountains or plains and later gave form to them building terraces,[54] ceremonial platforms, astronomical observatories, small dwellings, channels and canals, water fountains and basins, and, when it was needful, in certain chosen places they adopted the forms that were associated with the celestial prototypes, the constellations in the sky.

Because of this, the total design of these architectures of solid monumental masses was not made to be observed at first glance and from all places, but was meant to be seen only from pre-determined angles, usually from some elevated site where a vision of the whole complex was possible. Thus the apparently scattered groups of constructions that made up the complex blended visually with the mountains or the flatlands where they were built, and took on forms that sometimes showed themselves and sometimes were hidden from the view of the spectator in a permanent metamorphosis which defined them not only as objects of aesthetic contemplation but also as partaking of magical action.

---

(52) Eliade, 1985: 14-5 writes that according to Mesopotamian beliefs the Tigris River had its model in the star called Anunit and the Euphrates in the star Golondrina. He also informs us that there were celestial archetypes for the Babylonian cities: Sippar in the constellation of Cancer, Niniva in the Big Dipper. Correspondences between geographic spaces and the Milky Way are also found in the Path of Santiago (Europe), the valley of the Nile (Egypt) and, in America, in the Valley of Tepostlan (Mexico) and the Elky Valley in Chile.

(53) Molina (1573), 1943: 27

(54) Pachacuti (1613), 1927: 188

PISAC

Some thirty-two kilometers northeast of Cusco is where the Sacred Valley begins, and here one also finds the vast monumental area of Pisac.

Nearby, occupying a dominant position above the valley, there is a sculpture in the mountain which formation oral traditional has called *Inkil Chumpi* (the princess of the flowery skirt). The legend tells that since she was the only daughter and was to inherit all the lands of *Pisac*, the oracle at *Huancar Kcuichi* (parhelion)* destined her for marriage to the one who could build a bridge over the *Vilcanota* in just one night. Many were the rich and valorous pretenders to her hand, but only one, *Asto Rimac*, a ruler of the mysterious lands of the eastern forests, was her choice. Thus, covered by the mantle of destiny, which for this couple was the night, they set off - one to build the bridge and the other to invoke the spirits of the mountains under the strict admonition not to look at the prodigious task he was attempting. When she broke this promise, *Asto Rimac* disappeared, carried off by the turbulent waters of the river and with him went the possibility of establishing an alliance between the people of *Pisac* and the peoples of the eastern jungles. Ever since then *Inkil Chumpi*, turned into a ghostly figure of stone, rests up there alone, contemplating the valley of her ancestors.

---

*   Parhelion: a phenomenon of light that consists of the simultaneous appearance of various images of the sun reflected upon a halo of clouds around the sun.

The Condor, Messenger from the Sun

Built on top of a mountain and, in many sectors, right along the edge of an abyss, the archeological complex of Pisac is made up of various separate units; one just above the modern town corresponds to the ritual space of *Cuntur orcco* (Condor Mountain). Made up of groups of terraces and different constructions that are harmoniously integrated with the hillside where they are built, they form the outline of a gigantic condor at the moment of beginning its flight and the whole forms an allegory of the constellation of the Condor.[55]

The condor (*Vultur gryphus*) is the largest bird that is known and has a wingspan of more than three meters. With dark gray plumage and white markings on the wings, it has a bald head and its neck is circled by a collar of white feathers; the beak is slightly curved and it has thick feet. The bird has an imposing appearance, especially in flight, when it can reach altitudes of over six thousand meters above sea level. The condor is a scavenger and this habit caused it to be identified by the Andean people as the guardian spirit of the dead and it is associated with the peace to be found in sacred places.

In ancient times the condor was believed to be the messenger of the Sun and the one who was in charge of carrying the spirits of the dead on to the world beyond,[56] it enjoyed these attributes not only because of its majestic presence and high flight but also because its habitual abode is among the craggy cliffs on the highest mountains, where tradition says that Apus, guardian spirits, live.

Therefore it is no coincidence that the ritual space of *Pisac* is found between two cemeteries and with them as part of the total vision, this mythic being is symbolized in the act of carrying the spirits of the ancestors on his wings.

---

(55) Avila (1598) 1966: 162 says "...there are also some stars that are nearly all together. They call these the condor..."

(56) Cobo (1653) 1956 III:353, recorded the belief that the spirits of men who had lived well left their bodies when they died and were incarnate in the stars.

The Condor mountain and the town of *Pisac*.

Artistic representation of the characteristics of this monument, note how the terraces and the mountain form the figure of a condor.

In the area immediately above the condor is the quarter of the *Intihuatana*, named for a rocky area that has been carefully worked and where there is a central rock with two gnomons which were used to define the changes of the seasons. Around it are altars built of fine stone masonry, water fountains and basins and a ceremonial platform; all this establishes beyond doubt that this was the administrative seat that controlled this part of the Valley and from here they carefully supervised the agricultural production in the impressive terraces on the surrounding hillsides and below on the valley floor.

Agricultural terraces

The Andean territory, considered one of the eight centers from around the world where agriculture originated, cradled peoples whose needs and agricultural vocation allowed them over time to develop numerous types of crops; this was due not only to the fact that there are so many different kinds of ecological zones in the rough geography of the Andes but also to certain agricultural practices and the creation of technologies such as terraces.[57]

This technology arose initially from the need for more areas to cultivate; areas that could also overcome the problems of water supply, erosion of the soil and unstable climate. Once the Inca empire was consolidated, this technology became more sophisticated until it reached the high level which can be observed in the terracing in this valley.

---

(57) Terracing is a universal technology which is very old and is found in America and in Southeast and Central Asia.

Filled with different strata of stone, gravel, and agricultural soil, the terraces were built in places that were seen as pockets with micro-climates where there was less hail and wind; they were situated to receive the most sunlight. In synthesis the terraces were the result of "simplifying the natural ecological areas into a smaller number of artificial ecological areas that were more stable over time."[58] Therefore it was possible to obtain better harvests. It is calculated that the terraces of *Pisac*, including those on the valley floor, occupy some 65 hectares.[59]

Fitting the geometrical design to the natural forms of the hillsides and mountains, the terraces of *Pisac* not only solve practical needs but also respond to aesthetic, symbolic and religious motivation. In an Empire based upon the reciprocal relationships that were established with the leaders of the conquered peoples, some of the gifts that these chiefs received in exchange for their loyalty were small quantities of selected seeds from these agricultural areas, and these seeds had great prestige and were treasured not only for their quality but also because of where they came from.

(58) Earls, 1979: 119

(59) Santillana, 1999: 90

This technology along with a permanent system of irrigation, the selection of seeds and the establishment of a calendar for planting and harvesting (the product of continuous agricultural and astronomical observation) permitted them to acclimatize plants from the valley to areas that were higher up, and vice versa, and provided ideal conditions for the genetic control of species with the result that new and improved varieties were obtained. Such is the case of corn. In the area of influence of this valley seventeen varieties[60] were identified. Among them, one that grows between 2,800 and 3,300 masl. and is called *Parakay*, or Imperial White, is considered to be the type of corn that was the best of the genetic development achieved by the Incas.

Examples of this type of technology may be found by following the course of the river downstream through *Calca*, *Yucay* and *Urubamba* where in 1552 acclimatized varieties of peanuts, cotton, coca and hot peppers were recorded; and where the document of an ancient colonial notary published by M. Rostworowski made it possible to identify one of the oldest shrines in this Valley which was known as *Aquillay* and is seen in this photograph.

Believed to be a productive being and an intercessor with the rains, Inca tradition also connected the toad with corn seed and saw its celestial prototype in one of the dark clouds in the Milky Way just below the Southern Cross. Oral tradition associates these creatures with this mountain which, curiously, is connected with the terraces of *Moray* by a long rising path.

Since there are agricultural lands in the high parts of the valley (in the Andes the majority of agricultural land is found up in the higher zones), it was necessary to develop resistant varieties of corn that could be grown at higher altitudes.

MORAY

Six hundred meters above the valley floor, between 3,200 and 3,500 meters above sea level, its lands contrasting with what remains on the other side of the river of the green forests (4,000 masl) and vigorous vegetation native to the *Vilcanota* cordillera, stretch the reddish, semi-arid and saline plains of *Maras*. Barely irrigated by the water from a few springs, at one end of the plain there is one of the loveliest and most sophisticated environmental laboratories of the Inca state: *Moray*.

Moray was designed to take advantage of some natural depressions sunk like funnels below the level of the plain, the ruins are concentric terraces lining these hollows and there is a succession of ceremonial fountains in the largest of these terrace complexes. Contemporary studies have found variations in mean temperatures of up to 5°C on its agricultural surfaces.[61]

(60) Gade, 1967

(61) Earls, 1991: 68

75

The special characteristics of this sheltered place lead some to think that *Moray* was the center that made it possible to develop varieties of corn that were adapted to higher lands: varieties such as those that are cultivated today all around here and in other areas where before only tubers and grains such as quinoa were grown.

CHINCHERO

Low hills some 200 meters high separate the plain of *Maras* from the hills and plains of *Chinchero* (3,700 masl.). In this moderately cold territory, dependant for the most part upon rainfall, where once the cultivation of tubers reigned (more than three thousand varieties of potato have been identified worldwide), they also cultivated corn.

Shrines, an urban center and temples built on the top of a hill surrounded by terraces speak to us of the association between the cultivation of corn and the Inca state; the extensive lands that are planted in tubers and grains speak of an age-old agricultural technology. Here they plant mixed crops due to a complex ecology and the fluctuations in climate which occasionally damage some of the crops but leave the more resistant plants. This is why traditional wisdom in these demanding lands suggests that in order to maximize a surplus it is first necessary to think about minimizing losses.

So, spread out like a multi-colored weaving on these lands near *Chinchero*, there are parcels that today are planted with *potato*, *olluco*, *oca*, *quinoa*, fava beans and barley. They climb up the stairs of this geography but never reach the lands that are next to the glaciers, where finally only the bitter potato will grow and llamas and alpacas are pastured.

J. Murra called the model of ecological integration that is practiced by the Andean peoples "vertical archipelagos." That is to say the fusion of different altitudes into a unified system that is able to support populations. In the Andes this was the key which opened the door into the space occupied by the so-called high cultures.

Chinchero, Teteqaqa: On the winter Solstice its sculptured forms show the Sun in communion withe Mother Earth.

The Saltflats of Maras

The richness of the Sacred Valley was sustained not only by the fertility of its soils, the abundance of water and the benevolent climate, but also by springs of warm waters saturated with salt. This water was channeled to fill thousands of small shallow pools, that look like miniature terraces built onto the side of the ravine; this area, today known as the Saltflats of *Maras*, continues to produce appreciable quantities of salt through evaporation.

Its use was prohibited during the main purification rituals, and when these were over it was consumed with particular unction. During the festivities associated with the summer solstice, after offerings were thrown into the Sacred River (*Mayucati*) those who accompanied them in a rapid race until reaching the sanctuary at *Ollantaytambo* returned to Cusco bringing small sculptures of salt with them, each one, through its form (falcon, fox, toad), proclaiming the exploits of its bearer.[62]

Salt mines of *Maras*.

(62) Molina, (1574), 1943: 64-66

OLLANTAYTAMBO

View of the mountain of *Wakay Willca* (Tear of the Sun) which
is said to be the guardian spirit of this part of the Valley.

The terraces of *Muscapuquio*, located five kilometers
up the *Patacancha* River from *Ollantaytambo*.

The sanctuary of *Ollantaytambo*

View of the Temple of the Sun in the early hours of the morning
on the day of the winter solstice, June 21st. (southern hemisphere).

Located in the Sacred Valley some 89 kilometers to the northwest of Cusco, *Ollantaytambo* is one of the finest archeological complexes in Peru. Built on approximately 600 hectares, it contains religious, astronomical, administrative and urban complexes, with areas reserved for activities related to agriculture and livestock.

Choquetacarpo (the staff of gold), *Choquepayan* (where gold sprouts), *Choquepacarina* (the place-of-origin of gold), *Choquebamba* (the plain of gold), *Choquellusca* (where gold lies) are the names of some of the mountains and places that surround it. The religious and symbolic context of these names reminds us of the golden nature of this sanctuary.

Set in the midst of a geography whose mountainous conformation and random position, taken together with the extremes in the position of the sun along the horizon, *Ollantaytambo* permits a succession of astonishing luminous effects in its surroundings. This site, unique in the world, inspired many of the fantastic images of the Inca mythology. It also attracted the attention of priests and astronomers who wanted to establish in it the seat of the mythic origin of their rulers and consequently the spring of knowledge, which would make life in harmony with the Universe possible for all of the people included under the protective mantle of the Sons of the Sun.

To achieve this proposition it was necessary for them to synchronize the activities of man to the rhythms of earthly and celestial nature; rhythms whose intervals became translated in the word time, the knowledge of which was identified with the hero whose mythic history has already occupied us and with whose image, petrified in time, we will now concern ourselves.

Wiracochan or Tunupa.

Believed to be the messenger of *Wiracocha*, his fount, the pilgrim preacher of knowledge, the master knower of time, and described as a person with superhuman power, a tall man, with short hair, dressed like a priest or an astronomer with a tunic and a bonnet with four pointed corners, *Tunupa* was represented on one of the rocky flanks of the mountain called *Pinkuylluna* in a gigantic sculpted profile. In its details one can observe each one of the iconographic characteristics that are attributed to him. With a grim visage and an admonishing look, this face, worked by men and time, looks out over the abyss from the cliff that serves as his body upon which, nearly imperceptibly, they drew the hands that seem to support the load or bundle that a pilgrim carries.

Wiracochan or *Tunupa* a 140 meter high monument sculpted in the mountain; at the bottom of the photograph one can see the roofs in the town of *Ollantaytambo*.

Artistic composition of this figure and its iconography.

So here is manifest, as characteristic of this type of art, the particular need of the ignorant builders to make man's work the final expression of something that sacred nature had sketched out. However, the location of the basic morphology and the later work of conditioning its relief and forms was not due to simple chance but rather to patient study which resulted in a monument that is nearly mimetic, is harmonious with its natural surroundings, and also makes use of light and shadows to remind us of its supernatural nature. So let us see through this work the reason why this personage was held to be a master connoisseur of the world and time.

In the Andes the large number of interrelated ecosystems that are housed in this geography, coupled with an unstable climate, fostered through the ages the development of man's understanding and a body of knowledge directed toward finding the necessary means to sustain and create societies in harmony with the uncertain rhythm of its diverse nature; this is why they saw the world as a "living" and interrelated whole of which man is only one part.

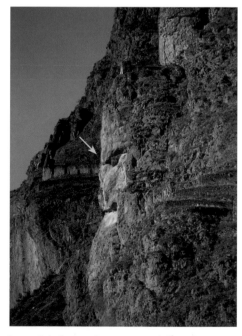

Art which has the virtue of capturing the spirit in its time, materialized and re-created this concept, providing this monument with effects of light and shadow which throughout the year show the hero in all his vitality, whether he be sleeping at 2:30 in the afternoon, or awake and vigilant one hour later.

So *Wiracochan* or *Tunupa* was the representation of the cosmic vitality of *Wiracocha*, a vitality that is none other than the synthesis of the way nature behaves. The meaning of his names shows this:

Wiracochan: Wiracocha's messenger

Tunupa: the canopy of the tree (protective Nature)
    its evil commanded; bold, impudent (unruly Nature)[63]

If indeed in these lands there are periods of a certain climatic stability (protective Nature) there are other circumstances in which the appearance of the Niño along the Peruvian coast provoke grave disturbances in the weather, with destruction and hunger as the consequence (unruly Nature; seismic activity is also part of this aspect). It was not chance that associated *Tunupa* with the sea, the forces of the earth and with volcanos.[64]

So the reasons motivating the development of techniques of dehydration are obvious, they were directed at finding ways to preserve food for long periods;[65] in time these techniques would consolidate the power of the Incas thanks to their establishment of an economy of storage on a massive scale and the subsequent redistribution of these products according to the interests of the Inca state.

This foresightedness associated with the civilizing message of Tunupa managed to define a system of production, treatment and storage, in maximum compatibility with the requirements of the environment. This may be seen in the area of the bundle that the pilgrim carries on his back (see pages 84 and 85); here, in the context of the symbolism of *Tunupa* as the knower of the world and provider of well-being, they constructed buildings designed to serve as storage facilities and there they deposited food and other products of man's industry.

---

(63) Bertonio (1612), 1879, II: 364

(64) The volcano near the salt flats of *Uyuni* (Bolivia) still bears his name.

(65) In the Andes nearly all known varieties of tubers, grains and meat are dried.

This permanent and urgent need to develop knowledge that was of the same manner and essence as the Nature was expressed in the chronicle of Blas Valera (1590) who commented: "The Inca priest was a personage who was respected by the great lords and the people. During his life he observed great abstinence since he never ate meat but only herbs and roots accompanied by his corn bread; he did not drink wine but only water, his home was in the fields, rarely in populated places; he spoke little, he dressed in a simple tunic of wool that reached down to his ankles and on top of that was a dark mantle, black or purple. His life in the countryside had as its object an easier contemplation and meditation upon the stars and the things of his religion..."

And since it is certain that nothing in the world can be planned without knowing about time, they set up landmarks and fixed points in order to study the movement of the celestial bodies.

Many of these landmarks were mountains which they held to be sacred because they were associated with the idea of being the axis of the world. Such is the case of *Pinkuylluna* (where the sculpture of *Tunupa* is carved) which was seen from the astronomical observatory today known as *Incahuatana*. Seen from that vantage point *Pinkuylluna* seems to be the axis around which the sun moves during the course of the year.

Sunrise over the peak of *Pinkuylluna* on the spring equinox,
seen from the *Incahuatana*.

Nevertheless it is not so easy to determine the date of a solstice through the simple observation of the extremes in the displacement of the sun in its apparent movement toward the north (winter) or to the south (summer). To accomplish this with more precision they took advantage of the phenomenon of the parallax[66] and built observatories. Using the peak of *Pinkuylluna* as a fixed point, from these observatories it was possible to establish a relationship between the first appearance of the constellation that protected corn (the Pleiades), viewed at the moment of its rising, and the position of the sun on the winter solstice. This technique in turn allowed them to determine the small variations in position among the stars, which occur as the years pass due to the phenomenon of precession of the equinoxes[67], and consequently this became a valuable instrument which made it possible to reform the calendar.

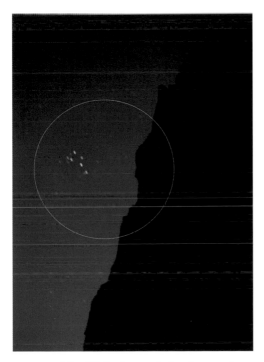 

The Pleiades and the Sun at dawn on the winter solstice (June 21st),
seen from the temple of the Sun.

---

(66) Parallax is the apparent difference that a star seems to have in the firmament due to a difference in the point of observation.

(67) Because of the retrograde movement of the equinoctial points (where the ecliptic crosses the equator), each year the seasons begin a little bit earlier.

Six months later on the summer solstice (December 22nd) they celebrated the most important festival of the empire (*Capac Raymi*), the coming-of-age ceremony for young men and the plants in the fields on this day the sun lit up the profiles of the mountain abyss to "illuminate" the head of *Tunupa* (corresponding symbolically with the idea of his being the one who "knows"), and then the light enters his temple while everything else around remains in shadow. (See photographs on page 91).

So the location of these buildings was not at random but just the opposite, it was due to the religious necessity of establishing a relationship through which various elements were bound together: man become stone in this world (*Kay Pacha*), the sacred mountain and the caves inside it where the mummies of the ancestors rested (*Ukhu Pacha*), and the sun which governs the world because it fixes time and lavishes life from the world outside (*Hanan Pacha*).

Drawing by Guaman Poma (1613) in which he includes *Pinkuylluna* mountain. It has several attributes, for which it was given various additional names such as *Aravipincollo uanca* (The protector of the music of the *pinkuyllo*) and *Cinca orcco* (The hill that masks). At the base of the drawing of the mountain one can read the word "*uacapuncu*" which means the door to the sacred space.

Sculpted profile of Tunupa and photos showing the effects of light produced in his temple during the summer solstice.

THE TREE OF LIFE

Pisonay tree (*Erytrina falcata*).

The Tree of Life

There are many peoples who have seen trees as the altruists of creation, and, in their solid and robust presence, a living testimony from the most ancient ages.

In the Southern Andes the word *Mallqui* was not only the word for the mummies of the ancestors, but also named trees, and the parts of the trees that were associated with the structure of the imperial lineages.

These Andean peoples, who had practiced ancestor worship from the very beginning, saw trees in the same way, and in the hundred year old roots they saw the sustenance of those trees under which the first men found protection and shade.[68] For them the trunk represented unity and the supernatural dwelling place of the spirits of their ancestors, the branches represented the noble lineages, and the fruits were the continuation of the generations.

Thus trees became symbols and figured in their myths along with mountains as the places where life found refuge when the great flood occurred. Trees also figured as *Pacarina*, origin places of some human lineages, and they appeared in the visions of priests as a two-headed serpent metamorphosed into an aged tree which then turned into a rainbow when it touched the sky (*Sachamama*).

Even at the end of the sixteenth century trees were the object of cult worship in the city of Cusco[69] as well as in the Sacred Valley; this was surely the case of the constellation of the split tree[70] which was represented on Earth in an unusual work built over the length and breadth of the alluvial fan where the modern town of *Ollantaytambo* is located. Here they created the figure of a tree divided into two parts by the flow of the *Patacancha* River. This design was described by Juan

---

(68) Garcilaso (1609) commented that in the Sacred Valley he had seen a great leafy tree which they held to be sacred because the Incas sat beneath it to witness the ceremonies which were held in the village of *Yucay*.

(69) Cristóbal de Albornoz wrote in 1613 that among the numerous shrines of the city of Cusco "Capa was a great tree which they dressed up and they made many offerings to it..."

(70) Oral tradition of the Aymara people recognized in the constellation of Aries their own constellation called *Ali Pakita* or Split/Broken Tree. Ibarra, 1982: 401

Santa Cruz Pachacuti (1613). When referring to the place where the *Inca Manco Capac* originated, he drew an ideograph and wrote:

"...And so the Inca ordered that they shoe the roots in gold and silver and told them to hang fruits of gold upon it because these two trees represented their parents *Apotambo* (the Lord of *Tambo*) and *Pachamamaachi* (Mother of the Time), and these were the trunk and the root, and the Incas who came after them were as the fruits. And all this was done to remember their greatness..."

At the base of this monumental complex (see photo and drawing) an unusual group of terraces has the appearance of tangled roots, and the trunk (outlined by the mountains of *Tamboqasa* and *Pinkuylluna*) takes on a twisted form through which the *Patacancha* River flows assuming the role of the life-giving sap which later is divided and shared through a network of canals like branches. These channels feed a succession of terraces where corn and quinoa are cultivated.

An important characteristic of this network of channels is that it separates from the central canal into two main branches, one goes to irrigate the *Hanan* section (*Hanan* - masculine, right) and the other, called Rainbow, leads to the *Urin* sector (*Urin* - feminine, left). In the Urin section a complex was designed and built to represent the fruit, this area shows characteristics that are elaborated in such a way as to make it a monument to the Nature and to the Time. The construction to which we are referring is none other than the pyramid of *Pacaritanpu* (A), also called House of Dawn or House of the Sun.

Indeed, fruits have a defined volume as one of their common characteristics, and so they represent the offspring as well as the origin that is contained in their seeds; the seeds in turn are charged with spreading the species throughout the world. Therefore, in the context of *Inca* mythology, this fruit was given the function of representing the *Pacarina*, the place where their leaders originated.

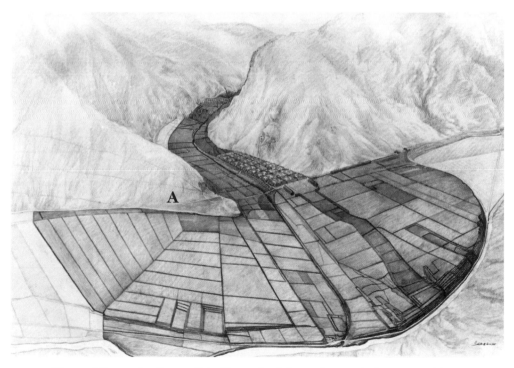

A

View of the majestic, mythic Tree of origin and an artist's composition.

An aerial photograph of *Ollantaytambo*; observe how the whole
complex forms the gigantic representation of the Sacred Tree. At the left,
representing the fruit, one finds the pyramidal construction of the *Pacaritanpu*
or the House of Dawn. (Photo: Servicio Aerofotográfico Nacional, Perú).

The Pacaritanpu, the site of the Inca's Mythic Origin

"Some five leagues distant from the city of Cusco is the *Pacaritambo*, which means Lodging of the Dawn or Palace of Windows, **which is much talked about and greatly prized more because of what they say about it than for its beautiful structure**, because it is such that it only serves as witness of its antiquity and now it is walled by trees which the natives believe are sacred, and the natives declare that from these dwellings the first Incas came out into the world after the universal flood." So wrote Cabello Balboa in 1586 without understanding the magnitude of the monument he was describing, because this place, that has recently been identified as an enormous structure in the fashion of a pyramid, was not built to be seen from the dwellings of man (from where one can only suspect its existence) but rather from the heights where the mountain powers have their abode.

And when we consider that one of the stages in the development of art in civilizations "was man's preoccupation with understanding the celestial universe and with developing systems that allowed him to understand and record its phenomena through means of an oral tradition, as well as a tendency to personify spiritual power and make it material."[71] Then we will understand the reason for each one of the special characteristics of this monument.

In order to apprehend it fully, it is necessary to climb above the valley, in this case we climb the mountain from which the construction was directed, until reaching heights which little by little show us how the complex of lines and planes that form the monument become visually more ordered as the observer continues to go higher and higher. Then the succession of nine terraces used for cultivation (and provided with irrigation canals and founts of water) appears to the observer to make up the two main faces of a pyramid; two areas that appear lower may be seen in the largest of these terraces, these are somewhat like "windows" directed into the Earth and symbolize the matrix of the origin of the Incas and of life (see pages 98, 99). Recent studies carried out in the area agree with a tradition that says that the soil for these terraces was brought from far away in order to build them, and pits dug for archeological investigation show the meticulous work done to position the stones to form the foundations; it is possible to see the successive levels of agricultural soil with which each of these terraces was filled.

---

(71) Grieder, 1987: 93

The pyramid of *Pacaritanpu* seen from one of the principal sites
for directing its construction, and an artist's composition
showing the general forms and sacred surroundings.

After five hours of continuous ascent and having reached the dwelling place of the mountain spirits, at a place called *Intipuncu*, or Gateway of the Sun, it is finally possible to see this monument in all its magnitude.

The shrine of *Intipuncu*, from here the pyramid of *Pacaritanpu* becomes manifest in the fullness of its sacred conception. Below: note the two enigmatic "windows" in this photograph.

In Inca mythology these "windows" symbolize the doorway through which one gains access to the world of the unknown. They also represent the sacred receptacles with which, by means of light from the sun, the upper world (*Hanan Pacha*) communes with the interior world (*Ukhu Pacha*) in the cycle that activates the principles of generation that give life to man and the Earth (*Kay pacha*).

In accord with this cosmology, at dawn on the winter solstice (June 21st) the day on which they commemorated the appearance of the Incas, a ray of light filters through the high mountains to enter the place where tradition said the Incas first entered the world as gods. Later the sunlight defines one of the edges of this pyramidal construction with astonishing precision, evidence that it was purposely aligned with the sun. Thanks to the information given to him by the astronomer Inca Juan Yumpa, the native chronicler Guaman Poma (1613) described this characteristic: "... And so in the planting, on the month and on the day, they look at the high peaks through which the sun rises and by the clarity of the ray of sunlight that gives onto the window, they plant and harvest food in this kingdom."

About this astronomer and his knowledge Guaman Poma also wrote: "This man had the order of philosophy, he knew about the stars and the circle the sun travels and he says that the sun sits on his seat and reigns there as a lord (June 21st), this same thing happens in August and in December.... and this clock does not deceive them, since for six months it moves along to the left and for the other six to the right." This effect can be observed in the photographs shown here.

From among the beliefs that were reaffirmed during the festivities fixed by this ancient calendar, one remains to this day in the soul of the common people. This is the spiritual concept of the Earth as the principal generator of life, which becomes activated in the first days of August, when it is time to begin to cultivate the soil and plant the main crop of the year. At this time offerings are made to show gratitude for goods and blessings received and yet to be received. This period, when the Earth receives peace because it is not being worked, and love because it is offered, is registered on this monument by a similar effect of light which occurs on the first day of August and is visible in the smaller of the "windows."

At dawn on the summer solstice (December 22nd) the sunlight
falls in the west face of *Pacaritanpu*; the ripening festival was held
on this day to celebrate the coming-of-age for young men
and the plants in the fields.

All of the above, then, symbolically explains the name of this place as the House of Dawn and the place where the Incas and time originated.

The Constellation of the Llama

The llama is the largest of the animals of the genus camelus native to South America. It stands a meter and a half tall and has a body that is approximately as long as well. The llama has a svelte appearance and is covered by woolen fiber that may be black, brown, gray or white and is used for making ropes and textiles. Domesticated in remote times, it was greatly prized because it can carry up to 20 kilos and can go for several weeks without drinking water as it obtains enough moisture from the damp pastures upon which it feeds. So in the vast territory encompassed by the empire of the Incas there was nowhere that the army went without being accompanied by thousands of these beasts of burden, under the everlasting presence of their celestial archetype, a constellation located just beneath the Southern Cross. It is made up of dark areas within the Milky Way plus the stars known to us as Alpha and Beta Centauri which serve as her eyes. Similarly, the llama was described in the histories collected by the Spanish chroniclers, among them we quote Bernabé Cobo, who reported: "...And they worship another which walks near the star of Urcuchillay and they call her Catachillay, which is something large next to another smaller one, they say that these are a llama next to her baby..."

In order to have her image in the Sacred Valley, a temple which represented the llama was built on the flanks of *Tamboqasa* mountain in *Ollantaytambo*.

In the architectural design of this ritual space one may see how its form tends toward the geometrical, as if the builders wanted to make it abstract so as to achieve a certain separation from the physical quality of the object and thus extract something simple from the amorphous.

There also exists a whole synthesis that reflects a desire to create a visual unity out of many elements and at the same time a formal necessity that derives from the desire to show as well as to hide a content which is essentially vitalist,[72] because as is characteristic in most examples of Inca architecture, the elements escape from the processes of repetition and seek to mould the phenomenological world in the representation of the symbol.

The main entrance to the Temple of the Sun; note how during the spring equinox (September 23rd) the protuberances worked in the blocks not only give it an additional aesthetic value but also, with the alignment of the shadows they project, they sanctity the lintel and fix the date.

_____

(72) From the perspective of the of art history it is held that vitalism is the actual force of life, and as such can manifest itself in human and animal form and even in abstract decorations. So wherever magical rites are associated with these forms, vitality, more than beauty, is the dominant aesthetic quality.

A ritual space dedicated to the Constellation of the *Llama*, seen from below.

A drawing of the temple dedicated to *Catachillay*, the Sidereal *Llama*.

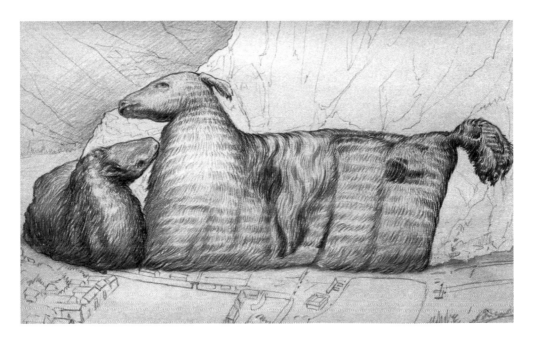

In the photos as well as in the drawing one can see how these constructions and the lines traced to create the form of the constellation retain the proportions that reproduce her, and in her symbolical context she shows her indissoluble relationship with water. Not in vain did a profuse Andean mythology hold that these animals were the creators of springs and lakes; it is thus that one finds the so-called Temple of the Sun (A) in the section which represents the head of the animal, while nearby there is a four-sided construction that is associated with a canal and various liturgical founts. This symbolizes the mother llama's eye (B).

The section that corresponds to her back is defined by a footpath that now connects the head to the tail, and the rest of her body is formed by the stairs and the terraces that represent the woolen fibers of her abundant coat. Curiously, at the base of the buildings (C) and (D) which were built to serve as storehouses for seeds and which also implicitly represented the reproductive organs (masculine as well as feminine), there are underground channels which, like urinary canals, discharged waters into the canals that irrigate these sections, in direct allusion to the mythological attributes assigned to her in her function as the divinity in charge of maintaining the precarious balance of the water cycle. Then one understands the version of the chronicles reported by Cobo (1653) which says that: "... a great river runs through the middle of the sky, which is a white ribbon called the Milky Way. It was believed that the llama would drink the water of this river and then she would let it fall down onto the earth..."

This version of the myth about the Celestial Llama, which was collected and transcribed by Francisco de Avila in 1598, helps to unravel the mystery that until recently surrounded the construction of this temple, and to ratify its unequivocal astronomical orientation.

"...they say that the yacana (*Catachillay*) is like the shadow of a llama or a double of this animal that walks through the center of the sky. She is very large and darker than the night sky, she has a long neck and two eyes... they also say that she goes down at midnight to drink the water of the sea, and then it is no longer possible to see her and feel her because if she did not drink this water the whole world would become flooded and they say that she has a baby and when that one begins to nurse, she awakens..."

This part of the mythical story was ingeniously expressed through the space that represents the llama's eye. Here it is possible to see a startling luminous effect which surely was measured with the precision sought by those who planned its construction.

The fact that this section of the temple is the only part that is lit by the sun is interpreted as the moment when, according to the myth, this animal from the sky symbolically "awakens". That is to say that after the constellation of the llama gets to its highest position in the sky during the month of April, it begins to experience slight changes in its position. Even greater changes are noticeable beginning in June, until it reaches its lowest position with respect to the horizon in October, when the rainy season begins, and then finally it is no longer possible to see the stars which represent her eyes. At this time, according to the myth, the Llama drinks the water from the sea to keep the Earth from flooding. So the interpretation was that she wakes up in June, alerted by the fact that in that month it is extremely dry, and so she moves down to drink the water of the ocean so that the cycle may begin again.

This sequence shows the phenomenon of light that marks the winter solstice (June 21st) in the place that represents the llama's eye. Note how the sunlight enters only into the area of this building; in their mythological vision this symbolized the "awakening".

At the top of the complex six enormous blocks of pink granite are joined in long, delicate settings to create the superb frontispiece for the ceremonial platform which is called the Temple of the Sun.

The enclosure for the worship of water and on the opposite page a detail of the interior. In this space earth, water, air and fire were joined, marking the beginning of the revitalization of *Pachamama*, the Mother of Time and Space (winter solstice).

Tampuquiro, the city dedicated to corn

Corn (Zea mays) originated in the Americas and was domesticated primarily in Mexico and Perú. The oldest corn cobs in South America were found in Perú in the *Piki* complex (5,000-3,800 BCE); in time this grain would revolutionize the Andean societies thanks to the control of its cultivation and the creation of new varieties[73] that were used as tools for civilizing and controlling. Corn thus became an important element in their religious beliefs and was often used as a special element in the worshipe to the Nature, whether the grain itself was used or the drink that was prepared from it. This drink, called *Ajha* or *chicha*, served as an integrating element uniting men and villages during festivals and ritual acts.

Corn was also worshipped and was included as an important element in the origin myths, among them are various versions that say that *Manco Capac*, the first Inca, was the first to plant in Cusco the sacred corn that came from the *Tanputtoco*, the *Pacaritanpu*.

Made sacred with the name *Saramama*, "Mother Corn," it was understood that this was the archetypal mother of production, and it is represented by ears of corn carved from stone and other materials; it was believed that "the soul or the spirit of the corn resided[74]" in these images.

With this same understanding a town was built which also defined a ritual space which some versions of the origin myth called *Tanpuquiro* or "palaces in the form of teeth." This place is none other than the ancient and still inhabited urban sector of *Ollantaytambo*, which presents an overall trapezoidal form similar to the shape of an ear of corn and in which the dwellings, occupying spaces known as "*cancha*", serve as the grains or "teeth". Curiously, grains of corn that are popped or toasted are also called *cancha*.

---

(73) Today it is thought that in America alone there exist more than 200 varieties of corn (Sanchez, 1966: 15), Perú has 55 varieties that are perfectly defined which makes it the country with the greatest variety and genetic diversity of corn. (Manrique, 1997: 119)

(74) Cavero, 1986: 174

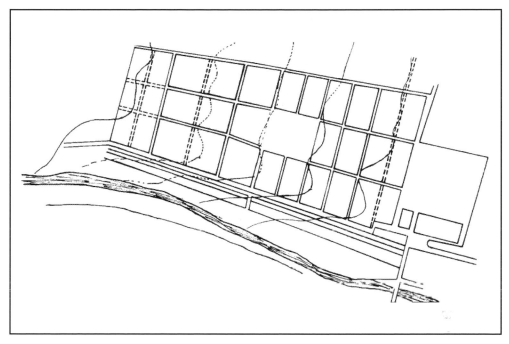

Urban plan of the town of *Tanpuquiro* or *Ollantaytambo*.

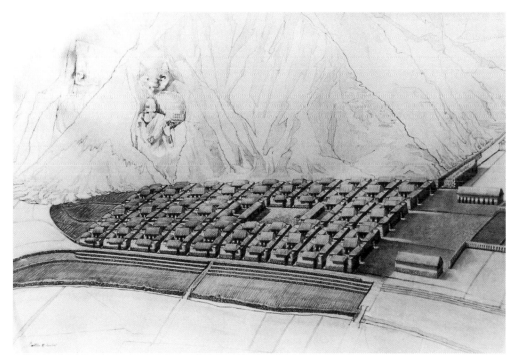

Artist's drawing of the ancient village of *Ollantaytambo*.

A great part of the political and economic power was concentrated in *Ollantaytambo* in ancient times because of the high production that was achieved on the broad extensions of land dedicated to the cultivation of corn. The possession of this cereal, so appreciated for its productive, food-giving and therapeutic capacity, allowed the political control of the subject peoples who received the surplus grain in redistribution. For this reason the greater part of the cultivation of corn was associated with the *Inca* state.

In the drawing it is possible to see that the town is divided into two sections: one is the high or "*hanan*" part (A) and the other the low or "*urin*" (B); both are further divided into five sections respectively, for a total of ten, which according to the origin myth was the number of *ayllu* or founding units of the town. Additionally the streets are oriented to the rising of the sun on the summer solstice. In the main part of this complex there used to be a plaza (C) which is now built over.

It is important to mention that the urban sector that corresponds to the lower part is the one that shows a better class of architecture, since all of its buildings have finer stonework and these buildings in particular have a double frame around the doorway in contrast to the simple entrances found in the upper part of the town. It is possible that this architectural difference was conceived with the intention of giving it a further similarity to an ear of corn since one can see that the bigger, more well-formed grains are found at the base of the ear.

Projecting from the base of the trapezoid is a series of buildings (D) which, representing the stalk, stretch down to the banks of the Vilcanota River (E) which symbolically nourishes it.

So they built a city dedicated to corn in order to feed themselves from the strength, vitality and magical power that were attributed to it, and in turn the inhabitants treasured in memory all that had to be done to cultivate it.

Ollantaytambo, the city dedicated to corn.

The Astronomical Observatory of Inticcahuarina

As was mentioned before, the prodigious development in the cultivation of corn in the Sacred Valley could only occur due to the establishment of a precise calendar for planting and harvesting. This allowed the establishment of periods dedicated to working the land in each ecological level. Calendars were established thanks to the development of observatory complexes such as the one we will now discuss.

There is little information provided by the chroniclers concerning the astronomical knowledge of the Incas, since the chroniclers made little effort to try to investigate the context of the information about the weather and climate of the Andes (for which the astronomer was the pillar); the subject was not very important to the majority of the Spanish because they thought it was a matter of superstition. Similarly, the justification for the process of (Spanish) domination that many of these writers gave was religious in nature, and for this reason this kind of knowledge held by the conquered peoples was systematically ignored. Nevertheless they did gather some valuable information which described the characteristics and basic principles of the way some of these astronomical observatories were used, as in this description written by Betanzos in 1551:

"The Inca ordered a certain thing called Pachaunanchango to be made which means the knower of time -which we may presume was something like a clock- and by means of this they determined when was the time to plant or harvest..."[75]

This information was confirmed by Fernando de Montesinos in 1644 who wrote:

"The Inca made a council of wise men and astrologers to punctually determine the solstices, using an observatory which was a kind of shadow clock, by means of these they knew which day was long and which was short and when the sun came and went between the tropics..."[76]

---

(75) Betanzos, 1551/1880: 101-102

(76) Montesinos, 1644/1957: 49

One of these devices, perhaps the most advanced in the Andes, is to be found in *Ollantaytambo* in the sector called *Incamisana*, and which we have named *Inticcahuarina* or the place from where one sees and understands the sun. Here the effects of light are not observed but rather those of shadow; the shadows make it possible to carry out more precise observations.

This observatory is worked in a solid mass of rock in which there are five brackets or protrusions sculpted in high relief and these project a series of shadows. These shadows change position as the sun varies its course throughout the length of the day and the year, but generally at midday they are located in the base of the whole unit; here there are carved modulations similar to steps and next to them are a series of notches worked in the living rock to define the spaces where the shadows position themselves, and this allowed the observers to define the different astronomical dates of their calendar.

We show two photographic sequences that illustrate these effects.

The first sequence was taken on the summer solstice (December 22nd). On this day the shadows begin a slow run from the first hours of morning to later project vertically onto the base of the rock, aligning themselves one with another at 12:00 noon, later they adopt a slight inclination which allows them to fit exactly into the notches cut for this purpose at 12:30. The date being determined by comparing the position of the shadows one day before or after.

A sequence of photographs of the observatory *Inticcahuarina*
observatory showing how they determined the summer solstice.

On the days when the sun crosses the zenith at this latitude (the 29th of October and the 14th of February) the shadow projected by a vertical gnomon casts a straight line beginning when the sun rises until it sets; this line passes through its own axis and at midday the sunlight falls straight down and the gnomon does not produce a shadow. At this time it was believed that the three spaces that structured the Universe were interacting; thus the sun was taking possession of all the worlds.

In the case of the horizontal gnomons which we were discussing, these were designed so that as well as their practical use (the date when the Sun passed across the zenith was determined through observing the entry of the middle shadow into the angle formed by the second and third steps), they also expressed their beliefs. So once the shadows become parallel they successively take possession of each one of the spaces in the stair sign, or the three worlds.

The *Huaca* of *Chimpaccahua*

The subject of the mythological universe in *Ollantaytambo* reflects through its contents the need to connect the existence of the world with an ordering principle, life-giving and fertilizing, such as the sun. Power and government depicted the sun as a vital element above nature, and since man's life requires order in the world, it was considered that the Incas or the Sons of the Sun should be the ones who supplied it. This notion of an integral connection between the Inca and the Sun is found summed up in the legend of *Chimpaccahua* or the man who looks straight ahead.

This legend recounts that at the beginning of times, the benevolent Nature that had cradled man was turned up-side-down, and the people were tumbled out into the world of darkness because they had forgotten Mother Earth. The oracle advised them that in order to turn this around, it was necessary to give her back all those gifts which they had received in the form of food. This they could do through the mirror of water in the mysterious lake of *Chaullacoccha*. In doubt and fear the men of the village refused to do this for her, but the Inca who ruled them ordered his own children do what the oracle said. Wanting to be sure that this happened, he climbed the mountain of *Pinkuylluna*, and there, once he had seen that the deed had been done, he remained, turned to stone. Only then the world recovered its color thanks to this man who at certain times shines like the sun.

"I we observe the general behavior of archaic man, we are struck by the following fact: neither the objets of the external world nor human acts, properly speaking, have any autonomous intrinsic value. Objects or acts acquire a value , and in so doing become real, because they participate, after one fashion or another, in a reality that transcends them. Among countless stones, one becomes sacred -and hence instantly becomes saturated with being- because it constitutes a hierophany, or possesses *mana*, or again because it commemorates a mythical act, and so on... Take the commonest of stones; it will be raised to the rank of 'precious', that is, impregnated with a magical or religious power by virtue of its symbolic shape or its origin."[77] This is what is meant by the *Quechua* word "*huaca*."

---

(77) Eliade Mircea, 1985: 12

119

This view shows one of the profiles of *Pinkuylluna* mountain where
one can see the stair-step design, and at the top of it is the profile of a man
with a headdress (*Huaca* of *Chimpaccahua*); the people who live
in *Ollantaytambo* today call it "The Inca's face".

At dawn on the winter solstice (June 21st) when
the Festival of the Sun, *Inti Raymi*, was celebrated, this face
from the legend becomes the Sun.

Because of all that was previously mentioned, the sanctuary of *Ollantaytambo* not only represented the cradle of the Sons of the Sun for the empire through its sacred conception and magical scope, but was also the final place chosen to bury the ashes of the cremated organs of the dead Incas,[78] since it was believed that when the life cycle of beings ended these rejoined the cosmos, returning by way of their places of earthly origin.

There also remained the ashes of the rebellion that was nourished upon her breast and which sought at the end of 1536 to retake the city of Cusco and to restore the rule of the Inca. When this attempt failed, Manco Inca (the fourteenth in the dynasty), finally abandoned this most precious sanctuary of an empire already in agony.

At this point, when the retreat to the craggy mountains where the cloud forest begins at Machupicchu and beyond down to Vilcabamba, he ordered the destruction of the roads and bridges; this strategy allowed them to resist until 1572, when the Inca was finally captured and decapitated in the city of Cusco; this was *Felipe Tupac Amaru I*, the last Inca.

Thus at the end the temples of this valley, which according to the Spanish chroniclers were enriched by Pachacutec, Tupac Yupanqui and Huayna Capac, entered into the twilight, and their buildings underwent the destruction wrought by man and the unrestrained ruin that always accompanies abandonment and time.

But this strategic isolation that permitted the Incas to resist during thirty-six years allowed Machupicchu, the most beautiful of the sanctuaries of this valley (since it had been abandoned for lack of supplies when the religious and state bureaucracy was broken), to remain protected for over thirty years, time enough to cover it with the green mantle of the Mother Nature.

---

(78) "The rites that they made for the Inca kings were very solemn, although prolix. The body of the deceased was embalmed, no one knows how: they remained so entire that they seemed alive... all of their insides were buried in the temple that they had in the town they called *Tampu*, downstream from *Yucay*." Garcilaso (1609), undated. Tome II:125

Traveling downstream along the Sacred Valley below *Ollantaytambo*, one finds numerous ritual spaces (some only discovered during the last century) which, like gigantic architectural sculptures, seem to form a series of ante-chambers leading to the most famous Inca sanctuary of them all: Machupicchu.

The complex at *Patallacta*.

Wiñaywayna.

MACHUPICCHU

Since it was presented to the world by Hiram Bingham in 1911, Machupicchu has exercised a power of fascination over all those who have visited the site, perhaps because in its architecture (which is one of the final expressions of the development of Inca art) it is possible to experience a space which, enhanced by the countryside that surrounds it, suggests the idea of the numinous or the infinite.

The Sacred Geography of Machupicchu

The *Yanantin*

In the information given by the chroniclers we learn that the sacred has a double called *huauque* or brother, just as the *Vilcanota* River is the double of the celestial River or Milky Way. This idea was contained in the word "*Yanantin*" which expressed corporal symmetry or complement and which at the same time was associated with the concepts of higher and lower, right and left, masculine and feminine.

In contrast to these complementary objects (*yanantin*), they also held sacred all that which was solitary or unique (*ch'ulla*). Garcilaso (1609) refers to this type of symbolism when he describes the conquest of *Cac Yauiri* by *Inca Mayta Capac*:

"All of these people, knowing that the Inca was going to conquer them, took possession of a mountain which is there in that region and is shaped like a loaf of sugar, just as if it were fashioned by hand, and it stands up since all the rest of the land around there is flat. They believed that this hill was sacred **because it was there all alone and because of its beauty** and they offered sacrifices to it..."

The conjunction of both of these symbolic elements (the single and the pair, odd and even) represented the unique whole that structured the order of the Universe. This whole was represented by the sign of the three steps, in which the three spaces that configure its form also represent the three major dimensions between which it was believed the vital energy flowed. And it was this energy that made the relationship between mankind and the divine possible.

This ancestral concept had an extraordinary influence upon the choice of the site where the highest work of the ideology of the Incas was built: Machupicchu.

The multiplicity of magical religious elements found upon her breast reaffirms the denomination as a sanctuary (without diminishing or lessening the political and administrative functions that this complex served), since these were conceived to satisfy the need to fix a final space that represented the far end of the Sacred Valley of the Incas. Because of this, its location necessarily had to be tied to the concepts that made this place sacred.

During the time of the Inca expansion the search for areas within the cloud forest that were able to provide a variety of food resources (among them coca), as well as the need for strategic sites that would permit the consolidation of their hold over these lands, supported a plan of continued penetration into the jungle along unlikely trails. One of these, known today as "Inca Trail", follows a route that leads through *Ollantaytambo*, *Patallacta*, *Sayacmarca* and *Phuyupatamarca*. This was probably the path that allowed them to discover a magical place set in the midst of a grove of high mountains and surrounded by an enormous serpent (symbolized by the Vilcanota River)[79] (see photograph page 128).

With respect to this symbolism the chronicler Ramos Gavilán (1589) said in referring to the temple of Coyatha, built on one of the islands in Lake Titicaca: "All of this temple was surrounded by an enormous serpent and they say that it was the water that was all around it..."[80]

We suppose that not only these elements impressed them but above all the sight of a natural representation of their socio-religious schema emerging from the Mother Earth.

Concretely we can say that the peaks now called Machupicchu and Waynapicchu represent a divine pair, a *Yanatin*, and facing them is *Putucusi*, a solitary peak, separate from the complex, standing alone like an axis, and completing the schema of odd and even. Taken together with the mountain called *Sachapata* they form a first circle.

---

(79) Sanchez, 1989: 81

(80) Ramos, 1589/1988: 45

Panorama of *Machupicchu* and its sacred geography.

In the surrounding area the mountains of San Miguel, *Cedrobambaorcco* and *Wayractanbo* form a second circle. On the tops of these peaks there are ceremonial platforms.

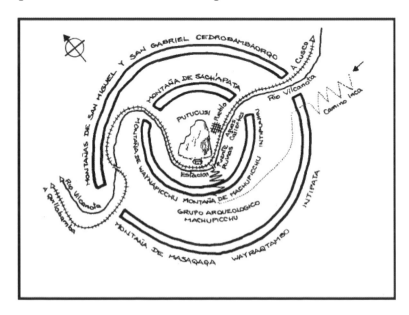

All of the geographic space described above was represented by two clear concentric circles carved in a flat rock which serves as an altar. This is found in the sector where a truncated pyramid is the base for the astronomical observatory of the Intihuatana. Here it is possible to observe how, during the dawn of the winter solstice, the sunlight consecrates the symbol associated with the geography of this site.

The Spirits of the Mountains

Today it is possible, when directed by the people who live in traditional communities, to learn the names of the guardian spirits that are associated with the shapes of certain mountains or particular natural formations.[81] Long ago these forms were shaped or prepared with some cultural elements so that they would really look like the forms they were meant to be, and in other cases the people designed temples and sacred spaces with characteristics so that the natural formations were adapted to the final design. These complexes generally are found in some accident of geography which generated propitious conditions of life for the community, such as lakes, hills, rivers, and springs; and these had a sacred connotation.

The basic fundament of their beliefs was a cosmic concept, a belief that the Nature and Time (*Pachamama*) was a completely alive generator of the vitality of all beings, animate and inanimate; these received their beneficial gifts through the spirits (*Apus*) which, manifest in the forms of the Nature, worked in a reciprocal correspondence with the acts of men.

These ideas determined the existence of a large number of entities to be represented, and among them a hierarchy of power was established, with specific functions in relation to their magical natures; Machupicchu is the final example of this idea.

The Custodial Puma and the Young Bird (*Wayna Pichiu*)

The mountain that is today called *Waynapicchu* presents a form that seems like a gigantic puma with its back curved and in an attitude of attack and defense. On top of the mountain some narrow terraces were constructed to represent raised hackles and these were used as productive agricultural areas associated with small enclosures and an altar for offerings and for the observation of the celestial vault.

---

(81) With respect to this, Cobo (1653/1956, IV:38) illustrated this ancient concept when he described the origin of the fourth *huaca* on the fourth *ceque* along the road to *Antisuyo*, about which he said: "the fourth huaca was a quarry called *Viracocha* where there was a stone that looked like a person and about which they say that when they were cutting the rock the figure came out from the rock and appeared just like that, and for that reason they worshiped it."

Next to this mountain there is another natural formation which consists of three rocky prominences; the two at either side represent half-opened wings and the one in the center, the head of a bird. In order to validate this idea and convert it into a cultural object they arranged small terraces to represent the ruffle on the condor's neck. This formation would have been named *Waynapichiu*, or young Bird. This name through extension and phonetic variation gives us the current name for the mountain - *Waynapicchu* (Young Peak).

The *Waynapicchu* Mountain assumes the form of a crouching puma and at the left one can see the bird.

131

When the characteristics of this impressive geography were evaluated (among them the existence of springs of water and quarries of white granite) and associated with the morphology of the mountains and their principal guardian spirits, which by themselves justify the importance of this space, it was decided to build here the complex that would become known as the most famous Inca sanctuary. Then a large number of workers began the labor of clearing the forest in order to prepare the area so that the architects, priests and astronomers could plan the construction of the whole complex, to the last detail, so that this place would occupy the extreme lower end of the Sacred Valley of the Incas and be its summation.

The symbolism of the Lizard of *Amaru Tupac*

In the Andean world for reasons still difficult to explain, the representation of flying lizards is found in nearly all the oldest cultures such as *Chavín*, *Pucara*, *Tiahuanaco* and *Inca*. Could it be that they represented the oldest being on the Earth? Or perhaps a mythical son of the waters, lord of land and air; generator of life, provider of food, mother of condors and of pumas, as it is possible to interpret the Tello obelisk from *Chavín*? (see the illustration on page 133).

So, too, ancient traditions registered in the chronicle of Juan Santa Cruz Pachacuti (1613), connect the birth of one of the sons of the Inca Pachacutec, who was called *Amaru Tupac*, in the place known as *Pumacocha* (the Lake of the Puma) with the mountain *Pachatuxsan* (the mountain that breathes, or exhales), which in its natural form appears to be a lizard; the chronicle says:

"So the news arrived that there had occurred a portent in Cusco and they told how a *Yauirca* or *Amaru* had come out of the mountain *Pachatusan*, this was a fiery beast of a half league in length and of two and a half spans in thickness with ears, fangs and whiskers and afterwards it sunk into the lake *Quibipay*, and then there came out two exhalations of fire.... of them they say that these were animals with wings, tails, four feet and spines along the back like a fish..."

Similar tales also connect this being with the harvest and the abundance of food stored in the granaries (*qolca*), because this creature spits into them and fills them.

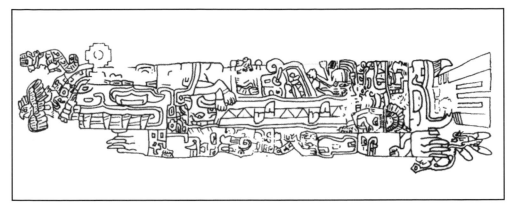

Drawing from the obelisk Tello of *Chavín*.

This supernatural being in its mythological and iconographic context was magnificently represented in a complex of buildings adapted to the topography of the site. Together they form a gigantic lizard whose design even included elements that represent the texture of its skin. Curiously this complex is found in front of the mountain that represents the condor and the puma in a position that is similar to that seen on the *Chavín* obelisk. (see photographs on pages 134, 135).

In the photographs and figures on the following pages it is possible to distinguish a series of terraces in the form of an ellipse (section A) that is similar to the shape of a reptile's head and for a curious observer it is possible to distinguish long rocks that, like fangs, stick out at the end of its perimeter. In the high part an enormous rock plays the part of the eye and crowning the lizard's head a natural rock sticks up that recalls the description given in the myth.

The section marked (B) corresponds to the center of assimilation of the nutrients of the reptile and this is where one finds the *Acllahuasi* (House of the Chosen Women). These women were dedicated to the weaving of fine textiles and the making of ceremonial utensils, food and drink. The building represents the back and thorax of the lizard, and here, also in a symbolic association, they built *qolca* (storehouses) for food as if they were part of the stomach of the animal. In the area marked (C) there is a sculpture of a condor associated with the cult of the dead and in the sections (D) and (E) the powerful legs of the left side of the animal communicate movement and give plasticity to the whole complex.

The Space of the *Amaru Tupac*

Built in the *Urin* sector in accordance with the system of division of ancient lineages in the Andes, this complex represents a flying lizard, which because of the characteristics of its design seems to be emerging from the waters of the *Vilcanota* River, to clamber unrestrained up to the top of the mountain where it remains petrified in full movement.

In this panoramic view of the ritual space of the lizard *Amaru Tupac*, note how the design seems to confer full movement upon the animal.

Artist's composition of the field and the powerful being
of the lizard represented at *Machupicchu*.

The Space of the Puma

In the Hanan sector which is across from the Urin, one generally finds the area dedicated to the activities of government. Here one finds the figure of a puma made up of a number of terraces built on the edge of an abyss and subtly designed with lines that transmit lordliness. He holds his head up and oriented toward the west and his body reclines in an attitude of rest and relaxation. Here, where the solar observatory called Intihuatana is located, the desing concept assigns to the pyramid the function of representing the head of the animal, the symbol of power, and in the part that corresponds to the back they built magnificent constructions; today one of these buildings is called the "Main temple" and the other is known as "the Temple of the Three Windows."

Photo and artist's view of the ritual space of the Puma.

The astronomical observatory of the *Intihuatana* and
the Temple of the Three Windows.

On the opposite side from this complex and near the top of the
system of water fountains, one finds the semicircular Temple of the Sun,
this is also where one finds the buildings with the finest masonry.

Representing the interior world; sculpted stair sings, niches
and appointments with an extremely fine finish are pound in the
hollow and rising above it (projecting up toward space
or *Hanan pacha*) is the Temple of the Sun.

Designed to withstand intense rains, the terraces as well as the buildings
known as the guardian houses of the agricultural sector hang from
the slope that ends on the edge of a profound abyss.

Dominating the surroundings at the top of the terraces that comprise the upper agricultural area there is a building whose view of the horizon invites contemplation.

THE ANCESTRAL BIRD

The complexes described above are grouped in a supreme whole which because of the singularity of its design makes this work a portent of abstraction, so handily and artistically controlled that, (seen from the top of Waynapicchu), it presents to the eyes of the observer the figure of a old and lordly condor as it flies toward the direction where night is born and the Milky Way disappears, toward the return to the origins, carrying with him the principal religious symbols, as if he were man's vehicle directed toward eternity and the infinite.

This lovely sanctuary of stone not only causes admiration because of its balanced architectural concepts and daring perspectives, but also because, together with the exceptional landscape that surrounds it, it re-creates a unique whole in which the geometrical work of man becomes the Nature. The whole complex is situated along the hidden crest of the Machupicchu Mountain, and is surrounded on all sides by precipices that fall away into the blue depths of the open spaces all around.

The Sanctuary of *Machupicchu* as seen from *Waynapicchu* is clearly defined as a condor in flight to the northwest.

Artist's conception of the sanctuary and the inverted image; here the characteristics and purpose of its design (bird in flight) are more easily seen.

The representation of this bird would also correspond to the image of a mythic being that a rich Andean tradition identified as the bird *Llulli*, and whose origin is now only perceived through legend. According to this story every time that men became dissipated or disordered the Sun sent a bird with iridescent plumage and the simple presence of this bird in the sky was enough to create a mysterious influence that ended the states of animosity, rebellion or war and produced love.[82]

(82) Portugal C., 1981: 59

Peace is the only sensation experienced in the magical atmosphere of *Machupicchu*.

There are many authors who have written innumerable works about this sanctuary, nevertheless there are few who have been able to feel the spirit of this place in its full dimension; among them Juan Larrea expressed it this way in "Machupicchu, City of Ultimate Hope":

"The traveler feels taken by a rare and unfamiliar euphoria. It is as if his mind suddenly triumphs, he wouldn't know how to explain the unexpected expression of wings...This illusive sketch of the kind of emotions that are felt in this place, which some may feel to be inexhaustible, explains why one is only secondarily interested in acquiring less mysterious concepts about the enigmatic city. The power of suggestion exercised by Machupicchu is inherent in its very presence."

Is Machupicchu really the name of this sanctuary? Would not its oldest name correspond to the form it represents, that is to say "Old Bird"?

The *Quechua* words *Machu Pichiu*[83] signify Old Bird, or the sovereign guardian spirit of peace among the mankind. Starting at *Pisac*, where the Sacred Valley begins, this bird, in the image of a condor, takes his flight norwestward to *Machupicchu*, at the end of the Sacred Valley, where the waters of the Sacred River spill away and from where the Celestial River, the Milky Way, is reborn.

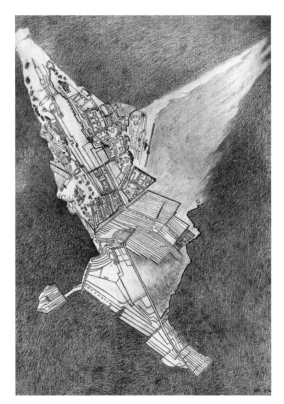

Plan of *Machupicchu* integrated with the artist's representation of the design.

(83) Gonzales H. (1608), 1989: 223

Waynapicchu.

145

The Flowers of Cusco and the Sacred Valley

The conjunction of beauty and the mysterious energy that permanently flows from the ruined remains of the works of those who once long ago sunk their hands into the earth or into one of the hundreds of mirrors of water that rest at the foot of the glaciers, lead us lightly up and down through the rugged forms of the high mountains. Among these colossi more than three of them pass the five thousand meter mark. At this altitude there is a mean temperature of 0 °C. Eight hundred meters lower the temperature is around 6 °C, while in the Valley that rests among the mountain folds the temperature is above 14 °C. Nevertheless because of the characteristics typical of this capricious geography and its respective climates, many species of plants grow here, each in places that despite being located at altitudes that correspond to colder zones not apt for the development of plants prosper in the small protected areas and niches that form a vast gamut of microclimates and flower during the rainy season, coloring the countryside with different tones and hues and comforting the spirits of those who travel in these steep places.

Hummingbirds on a poinsetta flower.

From down on the flat surface of the Sacred Valley at 2,900 masl. it is
(the town of *Huayoqari* is visible in the photograph) it is possible to see how crops
succeed one another up the mountain at short distances and upon reaching the limit
of productive altitude, these fields give way to narrow ravines at the foot of vertical
walls, while in the sheltered places the wild vegetation also prospers vibrantly.

List of the names of flowers:
Page 148 (from left to right)

1.
Gloxina sylvatica
Gesneriaceae

2. Alfilerillo
Geraniaceae

3. Panti
Cosmos peucedanifolius.
Compositae

4. Willcu
Ipomea
Convolvulaceae

5. Shinua.
Loasa grandiflora.
Loaseae.

6. Llaulli
Barnadesia horrida
Compositae

7. Lirio
Crynum americanum
Amaryllidacea

8. Yawuar taico.
Castilleja sp.
Scrophulariaceae

9. Tumbo
Pasiflora mollissima
Passifloraceas

10.
Bromarea sanguinea
Amaryllidacca

11. Chinchircoma
Mutisia acuminata
Asteraceae

12. Chiwanway
Crocopsis fulgens
Amaryllidacea

Page 149 (from left to right)

13. Angel tauna
Jatropha urens
Euphorbiaceae

14. Wakanki
Masdevalia
veitchiana
Orchidaceae

15. Supaicarco
Nicotiana glauca
Solanaceae

16. Sokca - Huscja
Astragalus
garbancillo

17. Waca waca
Halenia umbellata
Gentianaceae

18. Amapola
Papaver rhoeas
Papaveraceae

19. Granadilla
Pasiflora trifoliata
Pasifloraceae

20.
Sobralia dichotoma
Orchidaceae

21. Aya aya
Alonsoa acutifolia
Scrophulariaceae

22.
Gesneriaceae

23. Canaria
Echschlzia
californica
Papaveraceae

24. Sacha ñucchu
Salvia dombeyi
Labiatae

153

Page 150 (from left to right)

25. Chicchipa
Tagetes mandoni
Compositae.

26. Pirca
Bidens pilosa l
Compositae

27. Floripondio
Brugmansia aurea
Solanaceae

28. Boca de sapo
Antirrium majus
Scrophulariaceae

29. Hummingbird chickst.

30. Kiwicha.
Amaranthus caudatus.

31. Tarwi silvestre
Lupinus sp.
Fabaceae

32. Hummingbird eggs.

33. Qantuta, Qantu.
Cantua buxifolia
Polemoniaceae

34. Sunchu
Sonchus aleraceus
Compositae

35. San Pedro.
Trichocereus pachanoi
Cactaceae

36. Achira.
Canna edulis
Cannaceae.

Page 151 (from left to right)

37. Yawar chonqa
Oenothera rosea
Oenotheraceae

38. Rata rata
Abutilon molle

39. Nabo

40. Cardo
Silybum marianum
Compositae

41. Wallmi wallmi
Ageratina azangaroensis
Asteraceae

42. Muña
Minthostachys setosa
Lamiaceae

43. Gladiolo
Gladiolus cardinalis
Iridaceae

44. Pfalcha
Gentiana herrerae
Gentianaceae

45. Tancar
Solanum pseudolicioides
Solanaceae

46. Quico
Bidens andicola
Asteraceae

47. Qausillo
Siphocampylus tupeaformis
Campanulaceae

48.
Senecio comosus
AsteraceaeAsteraceae

Page 152 (from left to right)

49. Ayac zapatilla
Calceolaria sp.
Scrophulariaceae

50.Hummingbirds in
the nest.

51. Achancaray
Begonia sp.
Begoniaceae

52. Chawe-chawe
Paranephelius
uniflorus

53. Mutuy
Cassia hookeriana
Leguminosae

54. Hummingbirds
on a poinsetta
flower.

55. Michi michi
Cypalla herrerae
Iridaceae

56. Cardenal
Euphorbia pulcherrima
Euphorbiaceae

57. Margarita

58.
Hypseocharis
pimpinelifolius
Oxalidaceae.

BIBLIOGRAFIA

ANGLES VARGAS, Víctor. **Pacarectambo, y el origen de los Incas**. Industrial gráfica S.A. Lima, 1995.

ALBORNOZ, Cristóbal de. **La Instrucción para descubrir todas las Guacas del Pirú y sus Camayos y Haciendas.** En: UnInédit de Cristóbal de Albornoz. 8-39.Journal de la Societé des Américanistes.Tome LVI-1. París,1967 (1582-1584?).

ÁVILA, Francisco de. **Dioses y Hombres de Huarochirí.** Traducción del Quechua por José María Arguedas. Instituto de Estudios Peruanos. Lima, 1966 (1598).

BAUER S. Brian. **Avances en arqueología andina.** (Archivos de Historia Andina Nro. 16), centro de estudios regionales andinos "Bartolomé de las Casas" Cusco, 1992.
El Espacio Sagrado de los Incas, El sistema de Ceques del Cuzco. (Archivos de Historia Andina Nro. 33). Centro de Estudios Regionales Andinos "Bartolomé de las Casas",Cusco, 2000.

BERTONIO, Ludovico. **Vocabulario de la Lengua Aymara.** Publicado por Julio Platzman, edición facsimilar B.G. Teubner. Leipzig, 1879 (1612).

BETANZOS, Juan de. **Suma y Narración de los Incas, Biblioteca Hispano-Ultramarina.** Publicado por Marcos Jiménez de la Espada. Madrid, 1880 (1551),

CABELLO DE BALBOA, Miguel. **Miscelánea Antártica. Una Historia del Perú Antiguo.** Universidad Nacional Mayor de San Marcos. Facultad de letras. Instituto de Etnología. Lima, 1951 (1586).
Historia del Perú bajo la dominación de los Incas. Colección peruana Urteaga-Romero. 2da. Serie. II. Lima, 1920.

CALANCHA, Antonio de la. **Crónica Moralizada.** UNMSM. Lima, 1974 (1638).

CARRIÓN CACHOT, Rebeca. **El Culto al Agua en el Antiguo Perú.** La Paccha elemento cultural Pan-andino. Revista del Museo Nacional de Antropología y Arqueología Vol. II Nro. 1. Lima, 1955.

CAVERO CARRASCO, Ranulfo. **Maíz Chicha y Religiosidad Andina.** Edit. Universidad Nacional de San Cristóbal de Huamanga. Ayacucho, 1986.

CHANDLER, Daniel. **Semiótica para principiantes.** Ediciones AbyaYala. Quito, 1998.

CIEZA DE LEÓN. Pedro. **Segunda parte de la Crónica del Perú. Que trata del Señorío de los Incas Yupanquis y de sus grandes hechos y gobernación.** Edit. Jiménez de la Espada. Madrid, 1880 (1553).
La Crónica del Perú. Ediciones PEISA. Lima, 1973 (1553).

COBO, Bernabé. **Historia del Nuevo Mundo.** Notas y Concordancias por Luis A. Pardo y Carlos A. Galimberti. Tomos III y IV. Cusco, 1956 (1653).

CONDORI BERNABÉ /Gow Rosalind. **Kay Pacha.** Centro de Estudios Rurales Andinos "Bartolomé de las Casas". Cusco, 1982.

DEARBORN, David S.P. **The "torreón" at Machu Picchu as anobservatory.** Archaeoastronomy 5: S37-S49, 1983.

DOLLFUS, Olivier. **Territorios Andinos, reto y memoria.** Instituto Francés de Estudios Andinos. Lima,1991.

DONKIN, William. Agricultural Terracing in the Aboriginal New World.Viking Fund Publications in Anthropology 56.Werner Green Foundation, New York, 1979.

EARLS, Jhon. **Astronomía y ecología: La sincronización alimenticia del maíz.** En: Rev. AllpanchisPhuturinqaNro. 14:117-135. Instituto de Pastoral Andina. Cusco, 1979.
1991, **Ecología y agronomía en los Andes.** HISBOL. La Paz, 1991.

ELIADE,Mircea. **El Mito del Eterno Retorno.** Edit. Artemisa S.A, 1985.

ELORRIETA SALAZAR, Fernando; Edgar. **La Gran Pirámide de Pacaritanpu, Entes y Campos de Poder en los Andes.** Sociedad Pacaritanpu Hatha. Cusco, 1992.
El Valle Sagrado de los Incas, Mitos y Símbolos. S.P.II. Lima, 1996.

EVANS SCHULTES, Richard; HOFMANN, Albert. **Plantas de los Dioses.** Edit. Fondo de Cultura Económica. Mexico, 1982.

GADE, Daniel. **"Plant use and folk agriculture in the Vilcanota Valley of Peru A cultural historicalgeography"** .PhD Diss. University of Wisconsin, 1967.

GRANADINO, Cecilia. **Cuentos de nuestros Abuelos Qechuas, Recuperando La Tradición Oral.** Lima Graf. Lima, 1993.

GRIEDER ,Terence. **Orígenes del Arte Precolombino.** Edit. Fondo de Cultura Económica. México, 1987.

DE LA VEGA, Garcilaso. **Comentarios Reales de los Incas.** Tomos I, II, III. Edit. Universo S.A. Lima, S/f. (1609).

GONZALES HOLGUÍN, Diego. **Vocabulario de la Lengua General de todo el Perú llamada Lengua Qqichua o del Inca.** Edit. Universidad Nacional Mayor de San Marcos. Lima, 1989 (1608).

GUAMAN POMA DE AYALA, Felipe. Nueva Coronica y Buen Gobierno. Edit. A. Posnaski. La Paz, 1944 (1613?).

HERRERA, Antonio de. **Historia General de los hechos de los Castellanos en las islas y Tierra Firme de El Mar Océano.** Edit. Guarania. Buenos Aires,1946 (1601-1615).

HERRERA, Fortunato L. **Contribución a la flora del departamento del Cusco.** Universidad del Cusco,
Plantas que curan y plantas que matan de la flora del Cusco. Rev. Universitaria, Nro. 75. Universidad del Cusco, 1938.
Sinopsis de la flora del Cusco. Cusco.1941.

HEYERDAHL, Thord. **Aku – Aku.El Secreto de la isla de Pascua.** Edit Juventud. Barcelona, 1959.

HYSLOP, John. **"Qhapaqñan, el Sistema Vial Incaico".** Instituto Andino de Estudios Arqueológicos-Petróleos del Perú. Lima, 1992.

IBARRA GRASO, Dick E. **Ciencia en Tiahuanacu y el Incario.** La Paz, 1982.

LANNING, Edward. **Peru Before the Incas.** Prentice-Hall, Englewood Cliffs, N.J, 1967.

LARREA, Juan. **Corona Incaica.** Universidad Nacional de Córdoba. Buenos Aires, 1960.

LUMBRERAS, Luis Guillermo. **De los Pueblos, las Culturas y las Artes del Antiguo Perú.** Moncloa-Campodónico, Editores Asociados. Lima, 1969.

MARTÍNEZ Y MARTÍNEZ, Valentín. **Estudio Monográfico del distrito de Ollantaytambo.** Lima, 1966.

MOLINA, Cristóbal de, "El Cusqueño". **Fábulas y Ritos de los Incas. Las Crónicas de los Molinas. Los Pequeños Grandes Libros de la Historia Americana.** Serie I, Tomo IV. Lima, 1943 (1574).

MONTESINOS, Fernando de. **Memorias Antiguas, Historiales y Políticas del Perú.**En: Rev. Del Museo e InstitutoArqueológicoNro. 16-17:3-144. Universidad Nacionaldel Cusco. Cusco, 1957 (1644).

MANRIQUE CHÁVEZ, Pío Antonio. **El Maíz en el Perú.** Serie Tecnologías. Concytec, 1997.

PACHACUTI YANQUI, Joan de Santa Cruz. **Relación de antigüedades desteReyno del Pirú. En: Historia de los Incas y Relación de su Gobierno.** Colección de Libros y Documentos referentes a la Historia del Perú. Tomo IX (2da. Serie). Lima, 1927 (1613).

PARDO, Luis A. La Metrópoli de Paccaricctanpu. En: Rev. Arqueológica de la Universidad Nacional del Cusco, Nro.2:3-46. Cuzco, 1946.

POLO DE ONDEGARDO, Juan. **Informaciones acerca de la Religión y Gobierno de los Incas,** 2da. Parte. Colección de libros y documentos referentes a la Historia del Perú. Tomo IV. Lima, 1917 (1571).
Los errores y supersticiones de los indios, sacadas del tratado y averiguación que hizo el Licenciado Polo. En: Rev. Histórica Tomo I Nro. 1, 1906 (1584).

PONCE SANGINÉS, Carlos. **La ciudad de Tiahuanacu.** Facultad de Arquitectura. Universidad Mayor de San Andrés. La Paz, 1969 a.
El Templete semi Subterráneo de Tiwanaku, Acad. Nac. De Ciencias de Bolivia. Nro. 20. La Paz, 1969 b.

PORTUGAL CATACORA, José. **Danzas y Bailes del Altiplano.** Lima, 1981.

RAMOS GAVILÁN, Alonso. **Historia de Nuestra Señora de Copacabana.** Transcripción, nota del editor e índices de Ignacio Prado Pastor. Lima, 1988 (1589).

READ, Herbert. **Imagen e Idea.** Fondo de Cultura Económica. México D.F, 1975.

REINHARD, Johan. **Las Líneas de Nazca, Un Nuevo Enfoque sobre su Origen y Significado.** Edit. Los Pinos E.I.R.L. Lima, 1997.

RENDÓN, Maximiliano. **Leyendas del Valle Sagrado de los Incas.** Edit. Garcilaso.Cuzco, 1960.

ROMANO, Ruggiero. **Alrededor de dos falsas ecuaciones: coca buena cocaína buena; cocaína mala coca mala.** En Rev. AllpanchisPhuturinqa Nro. 19; 237-252.Cusco, 1982.

SANTILLANA, Julián I. **Andenes, Canales y Paisaje En: Los Incas, Arte y símbolos.** Edit. Banco de Crédito del Perú. Lima, 1999.

SÁNCHEZ CAMPOS, Hugo. **El Maíz, composición química y utilización.** Universidad Agraria. Lima,1966.

SÁNCHEZ MACEDO, Marino. **De las Sacerdotisas, Brujas y Adivinas de Machupicchu.** Lima, 1989.

SARMIENTO DE GAMBOA, Pedro. **Historia Indica.** Anexo al volumen IV de las obras completas del Inca Garcilaso de la Vega. Biblioteca de Autores Españoles, 195-279. Madrid. 1960 (1572).
Sociedad Protectora de la Naturaleza Cusco.
Plaza San Francisco. Jardín botánico de la flora nativa. Catálogo Cusco, 1988.

SULLIVAN, William. **El Secreto de los Incas,** Edit. Grijalbo. Barcelona, 1999.

TORERO, Alfredo. **Lingüística e Historia de la Sociedad Andina.** En: El Reto del Multilinguismo en el Perú, 51-106. Instituto de Estudios Peruanos. Lima, 1972.

URTON, Gary. **La historia de un mito: Pacariqtambo y el origen de los Incas.** En: Rev. Andina Nro. 1, 129-196. Centro Bartolomé de las Casas. Cusco, 1989.

VACA DE CASTRO, Cristóbal. **Declaración de los quipocamayos a Vaca de Castro.** Colección de Libros y Documentos referentes a la Historia del Perú. Tomo III (2da. Serie). Informaciones sobre el antiguo Perú. Lima, 1920 (1542-1608).

ZUIDEMAR, Tom. **The Ceque System of Cuzco: The Social Organization of the Capital of the Inca.** Leiden, 1964.
La imagen del Sol y la Huaca de Susurpuquio en el sistema astronómico de los Incas. En: Journal de la Societé des Americanistes. Vol. 63:199-230. París, 1974-1976.
Reyes y guerreros. Ensayos de Cultura Andina. Compilador Manuel Burga. Lima, 1989.

ZUIDEMA, R.T; URTON, G. **La constelación de la Llama en los Andes Peruanos.** En: Rev. AllpanchisPhuturinqa Nro. 9: 59-119. Instituto de Pastoral Andina. Cusco, 1976.